English
TWO

FOR COMMON ENTRANCE

Susan Elkin

GALORE PARK

AN HACHETTE UK COMPANY

Although every effort has been made to ensure that website addresses are correct at time of going to press, Galore Park cannot be held responsible for the content of any website mentioned in this book. It is sometimes possible to find a relocated web page by typing in the address of the home page for a website in the URL window of your browser.

Hachette UK's policy is to use papers that are natural, renewable and recyclable products and made from wood grown in sustainable forests. The logging and manufacturing processes are expected to conform to the environmental regulations of the country of origin.

Orders: please contact Bookpoint Ltd, 130 Park Drive, Milton Park, Abingdon, Oxon OX14 4SE. Telephone: (44) 01235 827720. Fax: (44) 01235 400454. Email education@bookpoint.co.uk Lines are open from 9 a.m. to 5 p.m., Monday to Saturday, with a 24-hour message answering service. Visit our website at www.galorepark.co.uk for details of other revision guides for Common Entrance, examination papers and Galore Park publications.

ISBN: 978 1 4718 6707 1

© Susan Elkin Ltd 2017

First published in 2017 by

Galore Park Publishing Ltd,
An Hachette UK Company
Carmelite House
50 Victoria Embankment
London EC4Y 0DZ

www.galorepark.co.uk

Impression number   10 9 8 7 6 5 4 3 2 1

Year   2021 2020 2019 2018 2017

Cover photo © donatas1205 /123RF.com

Typeset in India

Printed in Slovenia for Hodder Education, an Hachette UK Company

A catalogue record for this title is available from the British Library.

The Publishers would like to thank the following for permission to reproduce copyright material.

Photo credits

p5 © Artepics / Alamy Stock Photo **p7** © Peter S. Marble/ Fotolia **p10** ©Photodisc/ Getty Images/ World Landmarks & Travel V60 **p15** © arvitalyaa/ Shutterstock.com **p19** © Pictorial Press Ltd/ Alamy Stock Photo **p21 (top)** © Baloncici/ Shutterstock.com **p21 (bottom)** © Photodisc/ Getty Images/ World Commerce & Travel 5 **p29** © Ms Jane Campbell/ Shutterstock.com **p32** © Peter Cripps/ Alamy Stock Photo **p34** © chrisdorney/ Shutterstock.com **p38** © Flik47/ Shutterstock.com **p45** © KEITH MAYHEW/ Alamy Stock Photo **p47** © Axel Bueckert/ Shutterstock.com **p52** © Marco Maggesi/ Shutterstock.com **p55** © Fine Art Images/ Fine Art Images/ Superstock **p57** © Kevin Day/ Shutterstock.com **p58** © gemenacom/ Fotolia **p68** © Oleg Golovnev/ Shutterstock.com **p70** © Simon Bratt/ Shutterstock.com **p72** © Yevgen Belich/ Shutterstock.com **p75** © Denis Radovanovic/ Shutterstock.com **p76** © Mooshny/ Shutterstock.com **p82** © Ollyy/ Shutterstock.com **p87** © Steve Allen/ Shutterstock.com **p92** © 360b/ Shutterstock.com **p98** © Geraint Lewis/ Alamy Stock Photo **p101** © Slavko Sereda/ Shutterstock.com **p102** © The Granger Collection/ TopFoto **p112** © Everett Historical/ Shutterstock.com **p114** © Everett Historical/ Shutterstock.com **p116** © Jose Ignacio Soto/ Shutterstock.com **p124** © Mele Avery/ Fotolia **p127** © TheFinalMiracle/ Fotolia.com **p130** © Digital Vision/ Getty Images/ Astronomy & Space DV25 **p133** © Imagestate Media (John Foxx)/ Mature Perspectives SS15

Acknowledgements

Every effort has been made to trace all copyright holders, but if any have been inadvertently overlooked, the Publishers will be pleased to make the necessary arrangements at the first opportunity.

p4 Reproduced with permission of Curtis Brown Group Ltd, London on behalf of The Chichester Partnership. Copyright © The Chichester Partnership, 1938 **p5** 'La Belle Dame Sans Merci' by John Keats (public domain) **p17** *Cranford* by Elizabeth Gaskell (public domain) **p19** 'Goblin Market' by Christina Rossetti (public domain) **p20** 'If you drop litter, you're an idiot and must be punished' © Telegraph Media Group Limited 2014 (used with permission) **p27** 'I'm called little Buttercup' from *HMS Pinafore* by W S Gilbert (public domain) **p52** *Bleak House* by Charles Dickens (public domain) **p29** 'November' by Ted Hughes published by Faber & Faber Ltd (permission sought) **p30** 'November' by Thomas Hood (public domain) **p42** *Barchester Towers* by Anthony Trollope (public domain) **p43** 'My Last Duchess' by Robert Browning (public domain) **p45** 'Sweeney Todd Chichester festival theatre review' © Telegraph Media Group Limited 2011 (used with permission) **p55** *Lives* by Thomas North (public domain) **p55** *Anthony and Cleopatra* by William Shakespeare (public domain) **p56** 'The Wild Swans at Coole' by W B Yeats (public domain) **p69** From GRASSHOPPER by Barbara Vine (Penguin Books 2001). Copyright © Barbara Vine 2001. Reproduced by permission of Penguin Books Ltd. **p71** 'The Lotos-Eaters' by Alfred Lord Tennyson (public domain) **p73** 'Sacked over 'elf and safety, teacher who took two boys of 15 sledging as part of technology lesson' by Andy Dolan. Copyright © Daily Mail **p84** *Turbulence* by Jan Marks published by Hodder Children's Books (permission sought) **p85** 'We Are Seven' by William Wordsworth (public domain) **p87** From CLINGING TO THE WRECKAGE: A PART OF LIFE by John Mortimer (Penguin Books, 1983). Copyright © John Mortimer, 1983. 'Reproduced by permission of Penguin Books Ltd **p96** *Animal Farm* by George Orwell, published by Hamilton Books (permission sought) **p98** *Henry IV Part 2* by William Shakespeare (public domain) **p99** 'Gaddafi: tyrant or benign ruler?' by Reed Perry on reedperry.com (permission sought) **p100** 'Obituary for Gaddafi' © Telegraph Media Group Limited 2011. (used with permission) **p107** 'If you want to get nicked, get a hat' © Telegraph Media Group Limited 2006. (used with permission) **p110** *Birdsong* by Sebastian Faulks, published by Random House UK (permission sought) **p112** 'Dulce et Decorum Est' by Wilfred Owen (public domain) **p113** '100 Years Ago: Britain Enters The First World War' by Professor Stephen Badsey, University of Wolverhampton (university academic blog 25 July 2014) **p123** *Mansfield Park* by Jane Austen (public domain) **p124** 'Sonnet 116' by William Shakespeare (public domain) **p125** 'Why an arranged marriage 'is more likely to develop into lasting love' by Paul Bentley. Copyright © Daily Mail **p134** 'Date Expectations' in *The Times* (permission sought)

Acknowledgements

As always, I have to thank everyone at Galore Park Publishing for acting as collective midwife to this book.

Thanks are also due to my husband Nicholas Elkin, who scrupulously reads everything I write before anyone else sees it and is the best critic anyone could have.

Note to the teacher

English for Common Entrance Two is intended for pupils in Year 8 preparing for Common Entrance at 13+ and scholarship levels. It meets the requirements of the National Curriculum at Key Stage 3 and of the ISEB syllabus. There is also extension into off-piste learning and development – especially through wider reading.

Every comprehension activity – three in each chapter – leads pupils to use the text (fiction, non-fiction or poetry) as evidence for their answers.

The emphasis on reading offers plenty of opportunity for each pupil to develop his or her ability to read with discrimination and to express a response to reading.

Some of the chosen extracts are deliberately very challenging. Every teacher will have his or her own way of helping Key Stage 3 pupils to meet that challenge at an appropriate level and there are plenty of my thoughts and responses in the parallel *English for Common Entrance Two Answers*. And perhaps every teacher would do well to put, writ large, on the classroom wall T S Eliot's famous maxim: 'Poetry can communicate before it is understood.' No English teacher should expect pupils to understand, on first acquaintance, everything there is to understand about some of the finest writing in English. They are, after all, at the very beginning of a life-long learning adventure.

Users of this book will soon be progressing to GCSE, IGCSE or other Key Stage 4 courses – hence the introduction to topics like First World War literature and the multifarious functions of language which they will need in Years 10 and 11.

New to this edition are the 'Did you know?' sections, which should be used by pupils as an opportunity to practise crucial research skills.

Susan Elkin

Contents

Introduction

◯ Reading matters

Welcome to *English for Common Entrance Two*. If you have worked your way through Book One you will recognise the format. A newcomer to the series? Then I hope you enjoy the mixture of fiction, poetry, non-fiction and various sorts of language activity that each chapter offers.

I also hope that the recommendations in the 'Extra reading' sections will lead you to some books that you might not otherwise read – and that you find them as engrossing as I do. Don't be discouraged if you find some of these books are difficult to locate – try searching in your local libraries or in second-hand and specialist booksellers, including those found online.

There are many good reasons for being a 'bookaholic' (that's a neologism, by the way – see page 63). The first, of course, is that it's a great pleasure to bury yourself in a really gripping, interesting book. Another reason is that reading is a fine way of learning vocabulary, grammar and style. And any teacher will tell you that the more you read the better you will write and we all want you to sail through your Common Entrance examination. Bookish people tend to be very knowledgeable too because they are always effortlessly soaking up bits of information from their reading.

One of the important things to understand about English is that there are very few right and wrong answers. It's very different from, for example, maths. When you read a passage or poem you are quite likely to notice something new that teachers, pupils or the author of this book have not noticed before. Or you might read it in a different way so that your understanding is not the same as other people's. That can lead to very interesting discussions and is one of the great joys of studying English.

Remember, too, that you are probably reading some of these passages and poems for the first time. Several – Keats's 'La Belle Dame Sans Merci' (page 5) and the extract from *Mansfield Park* (page 123), for example – are very famous. You will almost certainly return to them and re-read them occasionally for the rest of your life – and, because you're an alert and thoughtful person, you will go on noticing new things. So don't expect to understand everything there is in a text when you first read it at school! The work you do there is the beginning of your journey of discovery, not the end.

Each chapter contains a section called 'Functions of language'. This is new for Book Two. It is an introduction to some of the many ways in which writers use language for a whole range of different purposes. I think you will find this an interesting aspect of English to study as well as helping to equip you for the forthcoming Common Entrance examination.

Alert, successful people are always curious. That is why I have included a short section in each chapter called 'Did you know?' to encourage you to develop an enquiring mind and to research things for yourself.

So – go on enjoying your work on this wonderful language of ours and the astonishing variety of fascinating texts that have been written in it.

Happy travelling!

Notes on features in this book

Exercise

Exercises are provided to give you plenty of opportunities to practise what you have learned.

Writing practice   Exercise

These exercises offer writing tasks that relate to the theme of each chapter.

> **Did you know?**
> There are interesting facts under 'Did you know?' that you can use as a starting point for practising your research skills.

> **Extra reading**
> These suggestions for further reading are linked to the theme of each chapter.

Progress further

At the end of each chapter, 'Progress further' contains interesting issues for you to research and discuss, specific ideas for reading and some creative activities.

> These notes highlight the ways in which language has changed over time.

Writing guidelines are available to help you with some of the writing activities. Look out for this box telling you where an activity is supported by guidelines. The writing guidelines can be found in *English for Common Entrance Two Answers* (ISBN 9781471867088), available separately.

1 Mysteries

A woman from the past

The narrator of Daphne du Maurier's famous 1938 novel *Rebecca* is curious about Rebecca, her husband's dead first wife. One day she explores an unfamiliar part of the house and discovers the mysterious Rebecca's bedroom.

I turned the handle of the door and went inside. It was dark, of course, because of the shutters. I felt for the electric light switch on the wall and turned it on. I was standing in a little ante-room, a dressing room, I judged, with big wardrobes round the wall, and at the end of the room was another door, open, leading
5 to a larger room. I went through to this room and turned on the light. My first impression was one of shock because the room was furnished as though in use.

I had expected to see chairs and tables, swathed in dustsheets, and dustsheets too over the great double bed against the wall. Nothing was covered up. There were brushes and combs on the dressing-table, scent and powder. The bed
10 was made up. I saw the gleam of white linen on the pillowcase and the tip of a blanket beneath the quilted coverlet. There were flowers on the dressing-table, and on the table beside the bed. Flowers too on the mantelpiece. A satin dressing gown lay on a chair and a pair of bedroom slippers beneath. For one desperate moment I thought that something had happened to my brain, that
15 I was seeing back into time and looking upon the room as it used to be, before she died … In a minute Rebecca herself would come back into the room, sit down before the looking glass at her dressing-table, humming a tune, reach for her comb and run it through her hair. If she sat there I should see her reflection in the glass and she would see me too, standing like this by the door. Nothing
20 happened. I went on standing there, waiting for something to happen. It was the clock ticking on the wall that brought me to reality again. The hands stood at twenty-five past four. My watch said the same. There was something sane and comforting about the ticking of the clock. It reminded me of the present, and that tea would soon be ready for me on the lawn. I walked slowly into the middle of
25 the room. No, it was not used. It was not lived in any more. Even the flowers could not destroy the musty smell. The curtains were drawn and the shutters closed. Rebecca would never come back to the room again. Even if Mrs Danvers did put the flowers on the mantelpiece and the sheets on the bed, they would not bring

her back. She had been dead now for a year. She lay buried in the crypt of the
30   church with all the other dead de Winters.

I could hear the sound of the sea very plainly. I went to the window and
swung back the shutter. The long shaft of light made the electric light look
false and yellow. I opened the shutter a little more. The daylight cast a white
beam upon the bed. It shone upon the night-dress case lying on the pillow.
35   It shone on the glass top of the dressing-table, on the brushes and on the
scent bottles.

I realised for the first time since I had come into the room that my legs were
trembling, weak as straw. I sat down on the stool by the dressing-table. My
heart no longer beat in a strange excited way. It felt as heavy as lead. I looked
40   about me in the room with a sort of dumb stupidity. Yes, it was a beautiful room.
Mrs Danvers had not exaggerated that first evening. It was the most beautiful
room in the house. That exquisite mantelpiece, the ceiling, the carved bedstead
and the curtain hangings, even the clock upon the wall and the candlesticks
upon the dressing-table beside me, all were things I would have loved and
45   almost worshipped had they been mine. They were not mine though. They
belonged to someone else. I put out my hand and touched the brushes. One
was more worn than its fellow. I understood it well. There was always one brush
that had the greater use. Often you forgot to use the other, and when they were
taken to be washed, there was one that was still quite clean and untouched.
50   How white and thin my face looked in the glass, my hair hanging lank and
straight. Did I always look like this? Surely I had more colour as a rule? The
reflection stared back at me, sallow and plain.

I got up from the chair and went and touched the dressing gown on the
chair. I picked up the slippers and held them in my hand. I was aware of a
55   growing sense of horror, of horror turning to despair. I touched the quilt on
the bed, traced with my fingers the monogram on the night-dress case, R de
W, interwoven and interlaced. The letters were corded and strong against
the golden satin material. The night-dress was in the case, thin as gossamer,
apricot in colour. I touched it, drew it out from the case, put it against my
60   face. It was cold, quite cold. But there was a dim mustiness about it still where
the scent had been. The scent of white azaleas. I folded it, and put it back
into the case, and as I did so noticed with a sick dull aching in my heart that
there were creases in the night-dress. The texture was ruffled. It had not been
touched since it was last worn.

Slightly abridged from *Rebecca* by Daphne du Maurier (1938)

Exercise 1.1

1 What is the narrator's married name?

2 Give another word for (a) swathed (line 7), (b) sallow (line 52) and (c) monogram (line 56).

3 Who do you think Mrs Danvers is?

4 Write a paragraph summarising what you learn about the narrator from this passage.

5 In what ways does Rebecca seem to have been different from the narrator?

6 What horrifies the narrator about Rebecca's night-dress and why? Use quotations from the passage to illustrate your explanation.

'La Belle Dame Sans Merci'

O what can ail thee, knight-at-arms,
     Alone and palely loitering?
The sedge has withered from the lake,
     And no birds sing.

5 O what can ail thee, knight-at-arms,
     So haggard and so woe-begone?
The squirrel's granary is full,
     And the harvest's done.

I see a lily on thy brow
10   With anguish moist and fever dew;
And on thy cheeks a fading rose
     Fast withereth too.

I met a lady in the meads,
     Full beautiful – a faery's child,
15 Her hair was long, her foot was light,
     And her eyes were wild.

I made a garland for her head,
     And bracelets too, and fragrant zone[1];
She looked at me as she did love,
20   And made sweet moan.

I set her on my pacing steed
     And nothing else saw all day long,
For sideways would she lean, and sing
     A faery's song.

25 She found me roots of relish sweet,
          And honey wild and manna dew,
    And sure in language strange she said,
          'I love thee true.'

    She took me to her elfin grot,
30   And there she wept and sighed full sore;
    And there I shut her wild, wild eyes
          With kisses four.

    And there she lullèd me asleep,
          And there I dreamed – Ah! Woe betide!
35 The latest dream I ever dreamed
          On the cold hill's side.

    I saw pale kings and princes too,
          Pale warriors, death-pale were they all;
    They cried – 'La Belle Dame Sans Merci
40   Hath thee in thrall!'

    I saw their starved lips in the gloam
          With horrid warning gapèd wide,
    And I awoke and found me here,
          On the cold hill's side.

45 And this is why I sojourn here
          Alone and palely loitering,
    Though the sedge is withered from the lake,
          And no birds sing.

John Keats (1819) [[1] A belt]

Exercise 1.2

Read the poem 'La Belle Dame Sans Merci' and answer the following questions:

1 Who narrates the first three stanzas of the poem? Who speaks the rest of the poem?

2 Explain in your own words why the knight-at-arms is 'Alone and palely loitering' (line 46).

3 What is the mood of the knight-at-arms? Quote from the poem to support your explanation.

4 How does Keats make the surroundings reflect the mood of the knight-at-arms?

5 Explain the meaning of (a) ail (lines 1 and 5), (b) steed (line 21), (c) thrall (line 40) and (d) sojourn (line 45).

6 Choose and comment on three words or phrases which interest you in this poem. What is the effect created by each one?

Easter Island

Easter Island, just fifteen miles long and ten miles wide, has 887 stone statues. Each weighs several tons and some are more than nine
5 metres tall. But nobody knows why or how they got there so they qualify as one of the world's great mysteries.

■ Statues on Easter Island

Easter Island, which belongs to
10 Chile, is in the southern Pacific Ocean and is one of the remotest spots on the globe. It lies 2,300 miles west of the coast of Chile and 2,500 miles south-east of Tahiti. The closest island is 1,400 miles away.

Imagine Easter Day, 1772, when a Dutch captain landed there. He was the first
15 European to set foot on the island, which at that time was virtually uninhabited. He and his crew were stunned by that, now famous, line of towering statues.

Scientists and others have tried ever since that first landing to solve the mystery of the statues. This is one theory:

Easter Island was inhabited by Polynesian seafarers who arrived in about 400 AD.
20 They had travelled thousands of miles in their canoes, guided by the stars, sun, ocean rhythms, sky colour, cloud formation, wave patterns and bird flight paths. For some reason they stayed.

This would tally with Thor Heyerdahl's work. A Norwegian explorer and scientist, Heyerdahl believed that the Polynesians sailed across the ocean in small craft.
25 In 1947, with five other men, he proved it was possible by building a traditional balsa wood raft and crossing the Pacific on it. The voyage took 101 days.

There seem to have been two classes of Easter Island inhabitant: those with long ears and those with short ears. The long-eared people were the rulers. The short-eared, who came earlier, were the workers. That is why, according to one theory,
30 most of the statues have long ears.

Not all the statues on the island stand upright or in line. Perhaps only a few made it to their intended destination while the rest were abandoned along the way.

The statues were carved out of the top edge of the walls of an inland volcano on the island. Once a statue was carved, it was rolled or dragged down to the base
35 of the volcano. Then it was raised by leverage with ropes tied around it.

The island's ancient grass, which has now almost disappeared because of over-grazing by herded sheep, was tough and could have been made into strong ropes. The theory is that the ropes were wrapped around the statue, which then functioned as a pulley. Two groups of men would pull first from one side and
40 then the other so that the statue inched forward.

It would have taken many laborious months, but a statue could have been 'walked' down to the ocean in this way. Each one which made it was placed in a line. They face away from the sea towards the centre of the island.

Some scientists think that if a statue fell over in transit, as often must have
45 happened, there was no way of lifting it again. So they simply returned to base and carved another one. That would explain why there are statues scattered about the island, not erected and apparently at random.

The sculpting and movement of these statues required the co-operation of the entire population of the island. So presumably there was a powerful religious
50 motive. The people must have believed with deep conviction that they were required by their gods to undertake this extraordinary work.

At its peak, the population of Easter Island may have been as high as 11,000. When the first Europeans finally arrived on the island, most of these people had died out.

55 Interestingly, ancient Easter Islanders could write and had their own unique system. No other Pacific Islanders knew how to write. Neither did American Indians.

Their diet poses unanswered questions too. Easter Islanders lived on sweet potatoes, which they farmed. Sweet potatoes originated in the Americas. How did the Easter Islanders get them? It is hardly likely that a few adventurous individuals
60 rowed or sailed 2,300 miles to Chile and returned with these vegetables.

Could Easter Island have been colonised by people from Chile? Probably not. DNA samples from graves on Easter Island have shown that these people were Polynesians, not American Indians. But Heyerdahl argued that the ancient Polynesians cremated their dead, which destroys DNA. He thought that the graves
65 found on Easter Island in modern times belonged to a later influx of Polynesians.

Researched and written by Susan Elkin (2006)

Exercise 1.3

Read the extract 'Easter Island' and answer the following questions:

1 Explain in your own words why the Easter Island statues 'qualify as one of the world's great mysteries'.

2 Give another word or phrase for (a) ocean rhythms (line 21), (b) leverage (line 35) and (c) colonised (line 61).

3 Why, according to one theory, do most of the statues have long ears?

4 What prompted Thor Heyerdahl to cross the Pacific Ocean on a raft?

5 What is puzzling about the diet of the ancient Easter Islanders?

6 Why do those who study Easter Island presume that the statues are religious in origin?

7 In a short paragraph, summarise how the statues might have been moved down to the sea from the spot where they were carved.

8 What is the problem with Easter Island DNA evidence?

Writing practice Exercise 1.4

1 Write an imaginary or factual account of visiting a mysterious place.

2 Using the passage in this chapter – and further information gained from elsewhere if you wish – write an advertisement for an Easter Island visit suitable for a Sunday newspaper or travel brochure. (See also Functions of language: the language of selling on page 25.)

3 Imagine you are La Belle Dame Sans Merci. Describe the encounter with the knight-at-arms from your perspective. You could write this as a prose story or you could make it a poem, perhaps using the same stanza shape as Keats.

4 Research and write an article about a real-life, unsolved mystery such as the finding of the *Marie Celeste*, the possibility that there was a female pope in disguise in the ninth century or what happened to the infant princes who died in the Tower of London in 1483. And there are many others. Gather your information from books and/or the internet.

5 Continue the story which begins in the extract from *Rebecca*.

6 Write in any way you wish about mystery.

These facts relate to the writers or topics featured in this chapter:

● *The Moonstone* by Wilkie Collins (1868) is generally regarded as the first crime mystery novel.

● John Keats died of tuberculosis in Rome in 1821 when he was only 26.

● Archaeological research is ongoing into how and why huge stones were brought from Wales and elsewhere to Salisbury Plain to create Stonehenge around 2000 to 3000 BC. Analysis of the rock types present at the ruin has recently provided new information about the source of the stones.

■ Stonehenge is a prehistoric monument in Wiltshire, England.

● Daphne du Maurier (1907–1989) lived most of her life in Cornwall and used it as the setting for many of her books, including *Rebecca*.

Exercise 1.5

Research and note three separate facts to add to the list above. They should relate to mystery, mysteries or to the writers and other topics touched on in this chapter, or perhaps link to your research to one of the Writing practice tasks. You should be able to summarise each of your facts in a single sentence.

Grammar and punctuation

Sentences

Remember that a sentence is a self-contained unit of communication. Think of it as a box with its capital letter at the beginning and full stop (which may be an exclamation or question mark) at the end.

Inside the box there is plenty of grammatical scope.

> Some scientists think that if a statue fell over in transit, as often must have happened, there was no way of lifting it again.

Here, the main verb is 'think': 'Some scientists **think** that if a statue fell over in transit there was no way of lifting it again.' 'Think' governs the two verbs 'fell' and 'was' which come in the subordinate clause signalled by 'that'. In addition to this, the embedded clause 'as often must have happened' is an extra and so it is marked off with a pair of commas within the main 'box'.

> In a minute Rebecca herself would come back into the room, sit down before the looking glass at her dressing-table, humming a tune, reach for her comb and run it through her hair.

Within this sentence Daphne du Maurier has linked five statements in a list, separated by commas. Rebecca would:

1 come back
2 sit down
3 be humming
4 reach for her comb
5 run it through her hair.

Each of these statements has a main verb (known as a finite verb) except 'humming a tune' which is a participle, part of a verb doing the work of an adjective.

When you construct sentences make sure you build a secure box. Then you can use other punctuation inside it if you need to.

This is a useful way of avoiding the very common and lazy mistake of ending sentences with commas.

Exercise 1.6

Punctuate these six sentences. Put in the capital letter and full stop first so that your outer 'box' is secure.

1 although he was frightened because he did not understand what was happening james opened the door firmly but quietly

2 did you really shout to frighten off any possible intruder as you entered the house switched on the lights and noticed that something seemed to be wrong

3 sit up shut up listen and take plenty of notes

4 in his novel bleak house charles dickens creates a character mr krook who dies through spontaneous combustion an unexplained phenomenon which has long fascinated human beings

5 all over the world there are statues in catholic churches and cathedrals usually of the virgin mary which people say they have seen weeping real physical tears sometimes of blood

6 daphne du mauriers best known novel dates from 1938 and although she wrote many others as well as some short stories and biographies nothing ever touched the popularity of rebecca except possibly my cousin rachel which was published in 1951

Changing fashions

Hyphens are **obsolescent**. That means that they are gradually disappearing from use. If they ever disappear completely they will be **obsolete.**

Today they are rarely used to link nouns or nouns and adjectives to make a different compound word. Generally we no longer hyphenate 'walking stick' (walking-stick), 'ice cream' (ice-cream) or 'sea cow' (sea-cow). We use far fewer hyphens than we once did, although we still use them in words like 'sister-in-law'.

Nearly two centuries ago when Keats wrote 'La Belle Dame Sans Merci' hyphens were usual in, for example, a compound like 'death-pale'. Even when *Rebecca* was written, around 80 years ago, hyphens were routinely used in words like 'night-dress' and 'dressing-table'.

Hyphens are still used occasionally by typesetters who have to break a word (between syllables) at the end of a line but most will try to avoid this clumsiness.

On the whole there is a trend today to use less punctuation rather than more so that a page of writing looks 'cleaner'.

Punctuation, like almost everything else, is affected by fashion. For another example, notice Daphne du Maurier's long paragraphs. Most twenty-first-century writers would use shorter ones.

See page 62 for examples of how hyphens are used to link phrases acting as adjectives.

◯ Spelling and vocabulary

ante- and anti- words

The narrator of *Rebecca* passes though an **ante-room.**

The Latin word for 'before' or 'in front' is *ante*. Notice that it is spelt with an '-e'. The room was like a hallway which led into another room.

The Latin word for 'against' is *anti*. So an antiseptic is a chemical which works against infection and an antitank missile is one which is fired at tanks and heavy machinery in war. Notice that it is spelt with an '-i'.

Exercise 1.7

Provide words to fit these definitions. Be careful to spell them correctly with an 'i' or an 'e':

1 Describes a device such as a burglar alarm, lock or intruder light.

2 Something which is third before the end in a list.

3 Describes events before the Biblical story of Noah's Flood.

4 The other side of the world to the UK.

5 Before birth.

6 Body of moving air of higher pressure than surrounding air so that pressure decreases from the centre.

Plurals

There is a clear rule for forming the plurals of words ending in 'y'. If the preceding letter is a vowel then the plural is usually formed by adding 's'. Thus:

toy	toy**s**
donkey	donkey**s**
affray	affray**s**

But if the 'y' is preceded by a consonant, the 'y' changes to an 'i' and add 'es'. Thus:

ovary	ovar**ies**
ability	abilit**ies**
poppy	popp**ies**
ruby	rub**ies**

Exercise 1.8

What is the plural of these words?

1 reliquary

2 decoy

3 plutocracy

4 refectory

5 tercentenary

6 foray

Now write a sentence for each word to show you understand its meaning.
You may use either the singular or the plural form. A dictionary will help you.

Like punctuation, spelling sometimes changes with time. Notice Keats's spelling of fairy as 'faery'. Actually, by 1819, 'fairy' would have been usual. Keats is using an old spelling because in 'La Belle Dame Sans Merci' he wants to create a poem with a timeless, romantic atmosphere. This will be explored in the next section.

Functions of language

Creating atmosphere

The atmosphere in the passage from *Rebecca* is sinister and full of suspense. Daphne du Maurier achieves this by:

- using a lot of detail to keep the reader waiting and to show us how the narrator is feeling
- using a slow pace – the incidents probably take longer to tell than they would to happen so the effect is like a slow motion film
- using 'jerky grammar', including some sentence fragments instead of conventionally correct sentences ('Flowers too on the mantelpiece.' 'The scent of white azaleas.')
- using short, very direct sentences interspersed with long ones ('The bed was made up.' 'Nothing happened.' 'The texture was ruffled.')
- using phrases breathlessly tucked into the ends of long sentences ('scent and powder', 'weak as straw', 'sallow and plain')
- appealing to the senses by emphasising sounds, especially the ticking clock and aromas or smells, such as the azaleas and the unwashed night-dress.

Keats creates an atmosphere of mournful longing and sadness in 'La Belle Dame Sans Merci' by:

- repeating soft consonants like 'l' and 's' ('alone and palely loitering'), a technique known as alliteration
- using long, slow sounds which sound like cries of pain ('made sweet moan', 'Woe betide')
- choosing old forms of words such as 'withereth' instead of 'withers', 'hath' for 'has' and 'thee' for 'you'

- using four-line stanzas which end with an abrupt, short, fourth line; most of these contain only single-syllable words which fall like hammer blows and sound very heavy and unhappy ('no birds sing', 'On the cold hill's side')

- including words with negative associations – 'withered', 'woe-begone', 'ail'.

Exercise 1.9

Write either a two-stanza poem or two paragraphs of prose. Take as your subject either someone who is frightened or someone who is deeply unhappy. Use some of the techniques detailed above to make your writing atmospheric.

> There are writing guidelines for this exercise in the answers. Look for the section at the end of the answers called 'Writing guidelines'.

◯ Speaking and listening

1 Prepare a reading aloud of any of the three passages in this chapter. Work out how to get the best out of the passage you choose. Perform it to the class or a small group. You might also record your work.
2 Work in a small group. Devise a ghost story that you can tell as a group. Then share your work with another group. Encourage feedback from the listening group.
3 Work with a partner. Discuss 'La Belle Dame Sans Merci' in detail. Do you think the poem is effective? Explain your answer.
4 Work with a partner. One of you is the narrator of *Rebecca*. The other is her husband, Maxim, whom she tells about her visit to his late wife's bedroom. Work out your conversation.

Extra reading

These books, stories and poems are either by or about the authors of the extracts in this chapter or they are about mysteries:

- *Rebecca* by Daphne du Maurier (1938)

- *My Cousin Rachel* by Daphne du Maurier (1951)

- *Daphne du Maurier* by Margaret Forster (1993)

- *The Woman in Black* by Susan Hill (1983)

- 'The Eve of St Agnes' by John Keats (1820) (this can be found in many anthologies and most selections of Keats's verse)

- *The Kon-tiki Expedition* by Thor Heyerdahl (1948)

- *The Truth about Celia Frost* by Paula Rawsthorne (2011)

- *The Mammoth Encyclopaedia of the Unsolved* by Colin Wilson (2000)

- *The Oxford Book of Victorian Ghost Stories* edited by Michael Cox and R A Gilbert (2003)

- *Fingersmith* by Sarah Waters (2002)*

- *The Woman in White* by Wilkie Collins (1859)*

- *Afterwards* by Rosamund Lupton (2011)

- *The Last Anniversary* by Liane Moriarty (2005)

*Recommended for very keen readers and for those taking scholarship

Progress further

- Read *Rebecca* (if you haven't already done so). Then read *Jane Eyre* by Charlotte Brontë (1848). Most critics are convinced that Daphne du Maurier was very much influenced by *Jane Eyre*. Work out why and decide how far you agree.

- Watch the 1940 film of *Rebecca*, directed by Alfred Hitchcock and starring Laurence Olivier as Maxim de Winter. It is now regarded as a cinema classic and will be in almost any DVD library. View it very critically. Decide why it was, and is, judged as a great piece of cinema. Or, if you disagree, work out your reasons. You might then write a review of the film.

- Research the life of John Keats. Prepare an informative wall poster for the classroom about him. The 2009 film *Bright Star* might help you.

2 Buying and selling

Community spirit

Shy, gentle Matilda Jenkyns, known as Miss Matty, has lost her money because her bank has gone bankrupt. In the fictional 1830s town of Cranford, her friends have persuaded her to open a tea shop to gain an income.

When we came to the proposal that she should sell tea, I could see it was rather a shock to her, not on account of any personal loss of gentility involved, but only because she distrusted her own powers of action in a new line of life, and would timidly have preferred a little more privation to any exertion for which she
5 feared she was unfitted. However, when she saw my father was bent upon it, she sighed, and said she would try, and if she did not do well, of course she might give it up. One good thing about it was, she did not think men ever bought tea. And it was of men particularly she was afraid. They had such sharp loud ways with them and did up accounts and counted their change so quickly! Now, if she
10 might only sell comfits to children, she was sure she could please them.

...

Miss Matty's sale went off famously. She retained the furniture of her sitting-room and bedroom, the former of which she was to occupy till Martha could meet with a lodger who might wish to take it. And into this sitting-room and bedroom she had to cram all sorts of things, which were (the auctioneer assured
15 her) bought in for her at the sale by an unknown friend. I always suspected Mrs Fitz-Adam of this but she must have had an accessory, who knew what articles were particularly regarded by Miss Matty on account of their associations with her early days. The rest of the house looked rather bare, to be sure – all except one tiny bedroom, of which my father allowed me to purchase the furniture for
20 my occasional use in case of Miss Matty's illness.

I had expended my own small store in buying all manner of comfits and lozenges, in order to tempt the little people whom Miss Matty loved so much to come about her. Tea in bright green canisters, and comfits in tumblers – Miss Matty and I felt quite proud as we looked round us on the evening before the
25 shop was to be opened. Martha had scoured the boarded floor to a white cleanness, and it was adorned with a brilliant piece of oil-cloth, on which

customers were to stand before the table-counter. The wholesome smell of
plaster and whitewash pervaded the apartment. A very small 'Matilda Jenkyns,
licensed to sell tea',[1] was hidden under the lintel of the new door, and two boxes
30 of tea, with cabalistic inscriptions all over them, stood ready to disgorge their
contents into the canisters.

Miss Matty, as I ought to have mentioned before, had had some scruples of
conscience at selling tea when there was already Mr Johnson in the town, who
included it among his numerous commodities. Before she could quite
35 reconcile herself to the adoption of her new business, she had trotted down to
his shop, unknown to me, to tell him of the project that was entertained, and
to inquire if it was likely to injure his business. My father called this idea of
hers 'great nonsense', and 'wondered how tradespeople were to get on if there
was to be a continual consulting of each other's interests, which would put a
40 stop to all competition directly'. And, perhaps it would not have done in
Drumble, but in Cranford it answered very well: for not only did Mr Johnson
kindly put at rest all Miss Matty's scruples and fear of injuring his business, but
I have reason to believe he repeatedly sent his customers to her, saying that
the teas he kept were of a common kind, but that Miss Jenkyns had all the
45 choice sorts. And expensive tea is a very favourite luxury with well-to-do
tradespeople and rich farmers' wives, who turn up their noses at the Congou
and Souchong prevalent at many tables of gentility, and will have nothing else
but Gunpowder and Pekoe for themselves.

Abridged from *Cranford* by Elizabeth
Gaskell (serialised 1851–1853)

[1] At this time it was against the law to sell
tea, which was heavily taxed, without a
licence – as with alcohol today.

Exercise 2.1

Read the extract from *Cranford* and answer the following questions:

1 Where is Miss Matty to live after the sale of her house and furniture?

2 Give the meaning, as the words are used in this passage, of (a) accessory
(line 16), (b) cabalistic (line 30), (c) commodities (line 34).

3 From the evidence in the passage, describe Miss Matty's shop in your own
words.

4 Which pricey blends of tea are well-off farmers' wives likely to buy?

5 What can you deduce about the narrator from the passage as a whole? Quote
from the passage to support your views.

6 What evidence is there in the passage that the townspeople have tried hard to
shelter Miss Matty from the 'disgrace' of having to become a shopkeeper?

'Goblin Market'

Morning and evening
Maids heard the goblins cry:
'Come buy our orchard fruits.
Come buy, come buy:
5   Apples and quinces,
Lemons and oranges,
Plump unpecked cherries,
Melons and raspberries,
Bloom-down-cheeked peaches,
10   Swart-headed mulberries,
Wild free-born cranberries,
Crab-apples, dewberries,
Pine-apples, blackberries,
Apricots, strawberries; –
15   All ripe together
In summer weather, –
Morns that pass by.
Fair eves that fly;
Come buy, come buy:
20   Pure grapes fresh from the vine,
Pomegranates full and fine,
Dates and sharp bullaces,
Rare pears and greengages,
Damsons and bilberries,
25   Taste them and try:
Currants and gooseberries,
Bright-fire-like barberries,
Figs to fill the mouth,
Citrons from the south,
30   Sweet to tongue and sound to eye;
Come buy, come buy.'

■ An illustration of 'Goblin Market' by Dante Gabriel Rossetti

From the opening of 'Goblin Market' by Christina Rossetti (1862)

Exercise 2.2

Read the poem 'Goblin Market' and answer the following questions:

1   What is remarkable about the diversity of fruit available in this market? What might this suggest?

2   Why are the words 'Come buy' repeated so often?

3 Find examples of the descriptions of the fruit appealing to different senses, and explain how they are effective.

4 What are the effects of the short lines and the rhymes? Use quotations from the poem to support your analysis.

'If you drop litter, you're an idiot and must be punished'

The only way to stop people dropping litter is to declare all-out war on them, says Alex Proud.

If you drop litter, you are a stupid, selfish, thoughtless yob.

This is my knee-jerk reaction to litter. The rural lane by my house resembles a kind of linear tip, with a fag packet, coffee cup or plastic bottle every few feet. The small parks near where I work in London look like supersize skips, filled with
5   fried chicken boxes. Even my own garden hosts a few plastic bags in trees, blown in from elsewhere. Every year it seems to get worse. I hate it, I hate people who litter and I think it's time we treated them like the antisocial slobs they are.

As I say, this is my gut reaction. But like all gut reactions, it's worth examining properly. Let's start with my perception that litter is getting worse – as people
10 always imagine things are getting worse. In fact it's actually worse than I'd imagined. According to a 2009 report by the CPRE[1] and the Policy Exchange, since the 1960s, littering has grown by 500%. Moreover, says the charity Tidy Britain, local authorities spend nearly £1 billion picking up litter every year.

It's true that a few people have attempted to reverse this rising tide of garbage.
15 A few years ago the author Bill Bryson tried to convince us to stop turning our green and pleasant land into an approximation of the town dump. He even suggested some fairly tough measures (although Bryson is so genial that he could make capital punishment for stealing bread sound pleasant). Alas, his nice-ish entreaties fell on deaf ears and our streets and parks and hedgerows are no
20 cleaner. So I believe the time has come to get nasty.

Before we do, though, we should ask ourselves if litter really is as black and white as oiks despoiling our country because they can't be bothered to walk five feet to a bin. Here, I did a little thought experiment comparing littering to a couple of other, similar blights – dog mess and graffiti. Not picking up after your
25 dog is disgusting, horrible and selfish. But I can sort of understand why you might not do it: carrying a bag of warm poo can ruin a pleasant walk in the woods. Carrying an empty Coke bottle, by contrast, is an inconvenience that is trivial to the point of non-existence. And graffiti? Most graffiti does ruin the

environment in a way that is similar
30 to litter – and more permanent. But
a small percentage of graffiti
improves the environment – and
the very best is art. Also, unlike
littering, the decision to tag a
35 motorway overpass involves
considerable effort and even
physical courage. Whereas littering
is just the abrogation of effort and
responsibility.

From an article written by Alex Proud and published in
the *Daily Telegraph* (2014)

[1] CPRE is the Campaign to Protect Rural England.
Bill Bryson was its president until 2010.

Exercise 2.3

Read Alex Proud's article which addresses the problem of litter – the waste product of consumerism.

1 Why does the writer call litter droppers 'slobs' and 'oiks'?

2 Identify and comment on some of the language he uses to persuade the reader that litter creates an unpleasant environment.

3 (a) What is the writer's point of view about litter?

  (b) How does he try to persuade the reader to share it? Quote from the passage to support your answer.

4 What does he argue should be done to prevent littering?

5 What factual evidence does the writer give to make his writing persuasive? Use quotations from the passage to support your answer.

6 (a) What else does he compare littering with?

  (b) What does he conclude?

Writing practice Exercise 2.4

1 Write a story in which someone is sold something unexpected.

2 Write a colourful description, using as many senses (sight, hearing, touch, taste, smell) as you can, to describe any market or shop known to you. Write your description as a poem if you wish.

3 Write a persuasive letter to a newspaper expressing strong views about the effect of pound shops on high-street trade or the use of piped music in shops. The purpose of your letter is to bring others round to your point of view.

4 Today, much selling and marketing takes place, not in shops and markets but over the internet. What experience of internet shopping do you, and perhaps your family, have? Is it a good development or not? Why? How do you think it will change in the future? Turn your thoughts and findings into an essay which presents various views about the changing face of shopping.

5 Write a short essay about the extract from 'Goblin Market'. Comment on the poet's style and use of words. The work you did in Exercise 2.2 will help you.

6 Write about buying and selling in any way you wish.

> **Did you know?**
>
> These facts relate to the writers or topics featured in this chapter:
>
> - Elizabeth Gaskell (1810–1865) was the wife of a minister in the Unitarian Church and campaigned all her life for what we would now call 'human rights'.
>
> - Christina Rossetti's brother, Dante Gabriel Rossetti, is well known for his flamboyant paintings of beautiful, idealised women and for being a leading member of the Pre-Raphaelite group.
>
> - Christina Rossetti, who never married although she had two offers, was deeply religious and worked for a while as a part-time nun.
>
> - The Council to Protect Rural England (CPRE) was founded by Sir Patrick Abercrombie in 1926 and in its 90 years has influenced policies on establishing green belts, town planning and litter.
>
> - eBay is a modern way of using auctioning, a selling technique which has been around for hundreds of years.

Exercise 2.5

Research and note three separate facts to add to the list above. They should relate to buying and selling, or to the writers and other topics touched on in this chapter. You should be able to summarise each of your facts in a single sentence.

Grammar and punctuation

Adverbs

Adverbs are words which modify (qualify) or tell you more about verbs or sometimes about adjectives, participles or other adverbs.

- I read Elizabeth Gaskell's novel **quickly.** (adverb 'quickly' modifying verb 'read')

- 'Goblin Market' is **colourfully** written. (adverb 'colourfully' qualifying participle 'written')
- Litter makes the countryside look **horribly** scruffy. ('horribly' revealing more about the adjective 'scruffy')

Most adverbs are formed from adjectives and end in '-ly' (e.g. quick/ quickly, colourful/colourfully, worrying/worryingly).

There are also many adverbs which do *not* end in '-ly' and they tend to be those words which can also be adjectives, nouns and verbs in other contexts.

Consider these sentences:

- He sat down on the bank. (Here 'down' is an adverb telling you more about 'sat' but it can also be an adjective in 'down side' or a noun in 'goose down'.)
- I ran fast. (Here 'fast' is an adverb modifying 'ran' but it's an adjective in 'fast train'.)

Exercise 2.6

Use each of the following words as adverbs in sentences of your own:

1	up	4	hard
2	over	5	later
3	well	6	around

Adverbial clauses of time

Groups of words containing verbs, known as clauses, can do the job of adverbs. Sometimes they answer the question 'when'? These are called **adverbial clauses of time**. Look at these examples:

- Mr Jones read *Cranford* **while he was travelling**. (Qualifies 'read'; tells us when he read.)
- **Before she died in 1894**, Christina Rossetti wrote many poems. (Modifies 'wrote'; tells us when she wrote.)
- **Since American Bill Bryson settled in England**, he has supported English causes enthusiastically. (Tells us more about 'supported', i.e. when he began to support English causes.)

Exercise 2.7

Add adverbial clauses of time to the sentences below. Such clauses usually begin with words which relate to time such as: since, while, during, before, after, as, once. Remember that each clause needs a verb of its own. Think about where to use commas within your sentences too. You may need one to separate the clause from the main sentence:

1 _____ Elizabeth Gaskell wrote poetry.

2 We read 'Goblin Market' in class _____.

3 My mother finished the week's shopping _____.

4 _____ I shall have a rest.

5 _____ Sam and Lucy will need their PE kit.

6 _____ litterers should be punished.

◯ Spelling and vocabulary

counter- words

The word 'counterfeit' means false, fake or forged.

The first part of 'counterfeit' comes from the Latin word *contra* meaning 'against'.

'Counterfeit' literally means 'made against' (the law).

Exercise 2.8

1 Using a dictionary to help you, list eight English words which begin with 'counter-' and write a short definition for each word

2 Choose another Latin prefix such as inter-, ad-, circum-, ab-, extra-, trans-, contra- or intra- and write a short list, with definitions, of English words which begin with it.

ang- words

Consider the following words which begin with 'ang-'. Notice that in some the 'g' is hard as in 'anger' and in others it is soft as in 'angel'.

angler	anguine
angiogram	angular
angst	angelology

Exercise 2.9

Match the words above to these definitions:

1 theory or study of angels

2 great anxiety

3 snake-like

4 x-ray image of blood vessels

5 fisherman

6 with sharp corners

Functions of language

The language of selling

The goblins in 'Goblin Market' use very specific language techniques. They:

- use a lot of imperative verb forms as if they were giving orders ('Come buy')
- make the product sound more attractive than it actually is ('Bloom-down-cheeked peaches')
- sound sincere and passionate ('Sweet to the tongue and sound to the eye')
- use language so fast and fluently that it confuses the customer. ('Taste them a try: Currants and gooseberries...').

Some advertisers will try to:

- trick customers into buying something that is more expensive than what they intended to buy
- mislead customers
- make their product sound better than it is.

There are currently laws which prevent advertisers deliberately misleading customers about a product within the UK and Europe, at least. Sellers are not allowed to browbeat people into buying things, or sign agreements without allowing them time to think, for example.

Nonetheless, many TV advertisements, roadside hoardings, notices in newspapers and magazines and all other forms of advertising use imperative verb forms. And they twist language to make their products sound more appealing than those of their rivals. Advertising slogans such as 'Beanz Meanz Heinz', 'Every little helps' and 'Think different' are interesting too. They use as few words as possible to say something catchy about the product which everyone will remember. People in the advertising industry are paid large sums to think up these slogans.

Exercise 2.10

Write an advertisement for one or more of the following new products:

- luminous shoelaces
- cake which makes you slim
- electric toenail clippers
- a holiday in a spacecraft.

Use the language of selling to make your advertisement as persuasive as you can and try to think of a good slogan to go with it. Looking back at 'Goblin Market' and the article by Alex Proud might help you.

◯ Speaking and listening

1 Working in a group, act out the scene in which Miss Matty welcomes the first customers to her shop.
2 Learn the extract from 'Goblin Market' by heart. Practise it until you know exactly how you want to say it. Then demonstrate your work to a partner.
3 Work in a pair. Take turns to tell each other about an occasion when you, or someone in your family, bought or were sold something which turned out not to be quite as expected.
4 Work in a pair. One of you is a customer in a shop selling perhaps shoes, flowers or jewellery. The customer should be as awkward as possible. The seller tries to deal with him or her.
5 In a group of three or four talk about the 'science' of selling (or 'marketing') – which can even be studied as a university subject. How moral do you think it is? Should there be more laws to control it?

Extra reading

These books or plays are either by the writers of the extracts at the beginning of this chapter or they have something to do with selling, shops and sales:

- *Words in the Dust* by Trent Reedy (2011)
- *A Single Shard* by Linda Sue Park (2001)
- *A Kid for Two Farthings* by Wolf Mankowitz (1953)
- *See It My Way* by Peter White (1999)
- *Death of a Salesman* by Arthur Miller (1949)
- *Hobson's Choice* by Harold Brighouse (1915)
- *The Hidden Persuaders* by Vance Packard (1957)
- *Mary Barton* by Elizabeth Gaskell (1848)
- *The Old Curiosity Shop* by Charles Dickens (1841)*
- Poems of Christina Rossetti – various books available*
- *The Grapes of Wrath* by John Steinbeck (1939)*
- *The History of Mr Polly* by H G Wells (1910)*

*Recommended for very keen readers and for those taking scholarship

Progress further

- The first Trade Descriptions Act was passed in Britain in the 1960s and there have been many laws to protect consumers since. Find out about these laws, using books and the internet, and consider how easy it used to be for buyers to be misled when making a purchase. What does *caveat emptor* mean?

- In this chapter we learnt about adverbial clauses of time. Adverbial clauses of place and manner work in a very similar way. Work out what they are and write some sentences using them.

- Read the song below aloud several times to get used to its rhythm. Now find out what music Sir Arthur Sullivan set the song to and what time signature the music has. You may need to find out more about the concept of time signature first. If you are seeking a challenge, make up a tune to accompany the song and figure out what time signature your tune follows.

'I'm called little Buttercup'

This poem is a song about selling.

I'm called little Buttercup – dear little Buttercup,
    Though I could never tell why,
But still I'm called Buttercup – poor little Buttercup
    Sweet little Buttercup I!

5 I've snuff and tobaccy, and excellent jacky[1]
    I've scissors and watches and knives;
I've ribbons and laces to set off the faces
    Of pretty young sweethearts and wives.

I've treacle and toffee, I've tea and I've coffee
10   Soft tommy[2] and excellent chops;
I've chickens and conies[3] and pretty polonies,[4]
    And excellent peppermint drops.

Then buy of your Buttercup – dear little Buttercup,
    Sailors should never be shy;
15 So buy of your Buttercup – poor little Buttercup;
    Come of your Buttercup buy.

From *HMS Pinafore* by W S Gilbert
(set to music by Sir Arthur Sullivan in 1878)

[1] Twists of tobacco soaked in rum and sold to sailors for chewing
[2] Soft bread usually in the form of fresh rolls
[3] Rabbits
[4] Cold smoked pork sausages (the word is a corruption of Bologna, the city in Italy where they were first made)

3 November

A November day

Charles Dickens (1812–1870) opens one of his most famous novels with a description of a November day in Victorian London.

Implacable November weather. As much mud in the streets, as if the waters had but newly retired from the face of the earth, and it would not be wonderful to meet a Megalosaurus, forty feet long or so, waddling like an elephantine lizard up Holborn Hill. Smoke lowering down from chimney-pots, making a soft black
5   drizzle with flakes of soot in it as big as full-grown snowflakes – gone into mourning, one might imagine, for the death of the sun. Dogs, indistinguishable in mire. Horses, scarcely better; splashed to their very blinkers. Foot passengers, jostling one another's umbrellas, in general infection of ill temper, and losing their foot-hold at street-corners, where tens of thousands of other foot
10   passengers have been slipping and sliding since the day broke (if ever this day broke), adding new deposits to the crust of mud, sticking at those points tenaciously to the pavement, and accumulating compound interest.

Fog everywhere. Fog up the river, where it flows among green aits[1] and meadows; fog down the river, where it rolls defiled among the tiers of shipping, and the
15   waterside pollutions of a great (and dirty) city. Fog on the Essex marshes, fog on the Kentish heights. Chance people on the bridges peeping over the parapets into a nether sky of fog, with fog all around them, as if they were up in a balloon, and hanging in the misty clouds. Fog creeping into the cabooses[2] of collier-brigs[3]; fog lying out on the yards, and hovering in the rigging of great ships; fog drooping on
20   the gunwales of barges and small boats. Fog in the eyes and throats of ancient Greenwich pensioners, wheezing by the firesides in their wards; fog in the stem and bowl of the afternoon pipe of the wrathful skipper, down in his close cabin; fog cruelly pinching the toes and fingers of his shivering little 'prentice boy on deck.

Gas looming through the fog in divers places in the streets, much as the sun
25   may, from the spongey fields, be seen to loom by husbandman and ploughboy. Most of the shops lighted two hours before their time – as the gas seems to know, for it has a haggard and unwilling look.

From *Bleak House* by Charles Dickens (1852)

[1] Small islands
[2] Huts for cooking and sleeping on the decks of:
[3] ships transporting coal

Exercise 3.1

Read the extract from *Bleak House* and answer the following questions:

1 What sort of weather is London experiencing? Use your own words to describe it.

2 What do the following words mean (a) tenaciously (line 12), (b) wards (as Dickens uses it here) (line 21) and (c) husbandman (line 25)?

3 Why does Dickens mention a prehistoric animal? Use quotations from the passage to support your ideas.

4 Explain why the phrase (a metaphor) 'compound interest' (line 12) is appropriate at the beginning of a novel which is going to be mostly about money.

5 How many times does Dickens use the word 'fog' in the second paragraph? Why do you think he repeats it so often?

6 What details or language choices show that this passage is set in the nineteenth century and not more recently?

'November'

The month of the drowned dog. After long rain the land
Was sodden as the bed of an ancient lake,
Treed with iron and birdless. In the sunk lane
The ditch – a seep silent all summer –

5 Made brown foam with a big voice: that, and my boots
On the lane's scrubbed stones, in the gulleyed leaves,
Against the hill's hanging silence;
Mist silvering the droplets on bare thorns

Slower than the change of daylight.
10 In a let of the ditch a tramp bundled asleep:
Face tucked down into a beard, drawn in
Under his hair like a hedgehog's. I took him for dead,

But his stillness separated him from the death
Of the rotting grass and the ground. A wind chilled,
15 And a fresh comfort tightened through him,
Each hand stuffed deeper into the other sleeve.

His ankles, bound with sacking and hairy band,
Rubbed each other, resettling. The wind hardened;
A puff shook a glittering from the thorns,
20 And again the rain's dragging grey columns

Smudged the farms. In a moment
The fields were jumping and smoking; the thorns
Quivered, riddled with the glassy verticals.
I stayed on under the welding cold

25 Watching the tramp's face glisten and the drops on his coat
Flash and darken. I thought what strong trust
Slept in him – as the trickling furrows slept,
And the thorn-roots in their grip on darkness;

And the buried stones, taking the weight of winter;
30 The hill where the hare crouched with clenched teeth.
Rain plastered the land till it was shining
Like hammered lead, and I ran, and in the rushing wood

Shuttered by a black oak leaned.
The keeper's gibbet had owls and hawks
35 By the neck, weasels, a gang of cats, crows:
Some, stiff, weightless, twirled like dry bark bits

In the drilling rain. Some still had their shape,
Had their pride with it; hung, chins on chests,
Patient to outwait these worst days that beat
40 Their crowns bare and dripped from their feet.

Ted Hughes (1960)

'November'

No sun – no moon!
No morn – no noon –
No dawn – no dusk – no proper time of day.
No warmth, no cheerfulness, no healthful ease,
5 No comfortable feel in any member –
No shade, no shine, no butterflies, no bees,
No fruits, no flowers, no leaves, no birds! –
November!

Thomas Hood (1844)

Exercise 3.2

Read the two poems called 'November' and answer the following questions:

1 What does Ted Hughes mean by (a) dragging grey columns (line 20) and
(b) glassy verticals (line 23)? What do these words tell you about the weather?

2 Describe what the narrator of Ted Hughes's poem sees in a ditch.

3 Choose and comment on two words or phrases which you find interesting in Ted Hughes's poem.

4 What does Ted Hughes's narrator see in the wood?

5 'Treed' and 'gulleyed' are unusual words to use in modern English. What do they mean and how effective do you think they are?

6 What does Thomas Hood's poem have in common with Ted Hughes's?

7 How do the two poems differ?

8 What does Thomas Hood's poem have in common with the extract from *Bleak House* at the beginning of this chapter?

November thoughts

The word November comes from the Latin word *novem* because it was the ninth, and penultimate, month in the Roman calendar. It is part of a numerical sequence which includes September, October and December.

Poets and writers have often written about November in gloomy terms. Alexander Pushkin, the Russian poet and playwright, writes 'A tedious season they await / Who hear November at the gate' in his 1833 play *Eugene Onegin*. The American/British poet T S Eliot (1888–1965) referred to 'Sombre November'
5 and the Scottish poet and novelist Walter Scott (1771–1832) wrote in *Marmion*: 'November's sky is chill and drear / November's leaf is red and sear.'

Perhaps it is because November has this dull, grey, cold image that its first week has, over the centuries, acquired a number of festivals and celebrations to brighten it up.

10 In 835 AD, for example, 1st November became All Saints' Day, once known as All Hallows' Day, in the Christian calendar. Saints – the famous ones and ordinary people who have done saintly things – are remembered on this day which is a public holiday in many European countries. Traditionally, the festival began the previous evening as All Hallows' Eve. And All Hallows' Eve traditions continue to
15 develop extensively, especially in America and Britain, although most of today's ghoulish fun and games are a long way from remembering, or praying to, saints.

All Souls' Day, also a public holiday in many European countries, falls on 2nd November. Known in Italy as the Day of the Dead it is a traditional time for families to remember people they've lost and to visit cemeteries. The Christian
20 Church regards it as a day to pray for the souls of all dead people.

In Britain, 5th November is Bonfire Night or Guy Fawkes Day. It was declared a public holiday by a decree of Parliament to celebrate the failure of the Gunpowder Plot in 1605. The plot, which was foiled at the last minute, involved a group of Catholics (Guy Fawkes became the best known) trying

25 to blow up the Houses of Parliament while the Protestant King, James I, was ceremonially opening it for the year.

■ A burning effigy on Bonfire Night in Lewes, East Sussex

30 Until 1859 parish churches were required to hold thanksgiving services on 5th November. Bells were rung and cannons fired during

35 the day. Effigies of the pope, Guy Fawkes and other hated figures were burned on bonfires.
Some of these traditions are still very strong – at Lewes in Sussex for instance. The bonfire, burning of the guy and firework display are usual in most places

40 although the day is no longer a public holiday.

Britain has far fewer public holidays than other European countries and many of those it has are clustered together in the spring: Good Friday, Easter Monday, May Day and the Spring Bank Holiday. Some people think we should have at least one new one at a different time of year.

45 Would early November be a good time for this? If so we have to decide whether to revive one of the old traditions or invent something completely new. Personally I'd go for 1st November for three reasons.

First, it is already a holiday in most other countries. If Britain prefers to avoid the Christian connotations of All Saints' Day it could simply be called, say, Autumn

50 Holiday or People's Day.

Second, most schools have a half-term holiday around late October or early November which means that a lot of adults take annual leave from work to be with their children. The new holiday could be incorporated into the half-term week and the date for half-term standardised as the Spring Bank Holiday week

55 at the end of May already is.

Third, it would launch November in a cheerful way and we might all stop being so negative about it.

Susan Elkin (2012)

Exercise 3.3

Read 'November thoughts' and answer the following questions:

1 What was the original meaning of the word 'October'?

2 What are the four adjectives that the poets use to describe November in the first paragraph?

3 Explain the meaning of (a) sear (line 6), (b) ghoulish (line 16), (c) connotations (line 49) and (d) standardised (line 54).

4 How do modern Halloween customs differ from old 1 November traditions?

5 Summarise the ways in which the celebration of 5 November has changed in Britain since 1605.

6 How does the writer think a new public holiday on 1 November could benefit British families?

Writing practice   Exercise 3.4

1 Write a story or poem entitled 'November'.

2 Imagine you are the sleeping tramp in Ted Hughes's poem. Tell your story.

3 You are an advice columnist in a magazine or newspaper. A reader writes saying that he or she finds November a very dull month and can think of nothing to do. Write your reply offering advice and giving ideas for how the reader might enjoy some of the delights of November.

> There are writing guidelines for task 3 (advice writing) in the answers. Look for the section at the end of the answers called 'Writing guidelines'.

4 Write the next three or four paragraphs to follow Dickens's description in the extract from *Bleak House* at the beginning of the chapter. Remember he is about to introduce some characters and/or action. Try to use his style if you can.

5 Write about November in any way you wish.

6 'How does Dickens make the opening of *Bleak House* interesting?' Answer this question as an English literature essay, developing your ideas fully and in a detailed and well-structured manner. Comment on Dickens's use of language and pick out phrases and words which you find particularly interesting. Explain why. Your answers to Exercise 3.1 will help you.

7 Write your views about public holidays in Britain. Should there be more? How should they be spaced during the year?

Did you know?

These facts relate to the writers or topics featured in this chapter:

- Ted Hughes was married to the American poet Sylvia Plath, who committed suicide in 1963. They had two children together.

- Topaz is the birthstone for November and the flower of the month is the chrysanthemum.

- Because the peace document to mark the end of the First World War was signed at the eleventh hour of the eleventh day of the eleventh month of 1918, 11 November has been observed ever since as Remembrance Day.

■ The Cenotaph in London

- Thomas Hood was a poet of the early nineteenth century who is known for his darkly comic verse and poems of social protest.

- Once Charles Dickens had become successful and well off he bought a house near Rochester in Kent where he lived and worked from 1856 until his death in 1870.

Exercise 3.5

Research and note three separate facts to add to the list above. They should relate to November or to the writers and other topics touched on in this chapter. You should be able to summarise each of your facts in a single sentence.

Grammar and punctuation

Modifiers

A **modifier** is a word or phrase which modifies, transforms, changes, alters, qualifies, determines or affects the meaning of another word or phrase.

Modifiers, which are sometimes called determiners, include various sorts of adjective and adjectival phrases, adverbs and adverbial phrases and possessive pronouns.

Consider these examples. The modifier is in bold.

She wore a hat.

   She wore **your hat** (possessive pronoun modifies 'hat')

   She wore a hat, **inherited from her grandmother** (adjectival phrase modifies 'hat')

We waited.

   We waited **quietly** (adverb modifies 'waited')

   We waited **in quiet respect** (adverbial phrase modifies 'waited')

Children laugh.

   Boisterous children laugh (adjective modifies 'children')

In each case the modifier changes the meaning of the sentence.

Modifiers are a large group. Think of them as a big grammatical 'file' into which many smaller files fit.

Exercise 3.6

Put modifiers (as single words or phrases) into the gaps in these sentences. (Note each sentence already makes sense but you are changing the meaning.)

1 Charles Dickens wrote _____ books.

2 November, December, January and February are _____ months.

3 Richard ate _____.

4 _____, Thomas Hood was _____ poet.

5 I like _____ poems, _____ plays and _____ fiction.

6 _____ modifiers are adjectives and adverbs.

7 Would you like to have _____ supper with us _____ ?

8 There is _____ difficulty here.

9 I like _____ cooking.

10 _____ music is _____ too loud.

Revision of apostrophes

Remember that apostrophes have two functions:

- They stand in place of omitted letters.
- They indicate possession.

Look at these examples from the passages at the beginning of this chapter:

- Omission
  - 'prentice boy (for apprentice boy)
  - they've (for they have)
- Possession
  - one another's umbrellas
  - the tramp's face
  - the hill's hanging silence
  - the keeper's gibbet
  - like a hedgehog's (hair)
  - Dickens's style

One of the worst and commonest mistakes is to use an apostrophe simply because the word is plural, or ends in an 's', for example, words used in the passages: snowflakes, services, bonfires.

Exercise 3.7

Put apostrophes in these examples where they are needed. In brackets after each put (p) for possession, (o) for omission or (n) for no apostrophe needed:

1 Thomas Hoods poems

2 dos and donts

3 novels written by Victorians

4 St Marys Church

5 the reigns of Stuart Kings and Queens

6 Queen Annes reign

7 six oclock

8 the witnesss statement

9 We shouldnt keep dogs and cats indoors too much.

10 the foxs habitat

11 *Guys and Dolls*

12 Aunt Glyniss house

Semicolons for lists

Look carefully at the punctuation in these sentences from *Bleak House*:

Fog creeping into the cabooses of collier-brigs; fog lying out on the yards, and hovering in the rigging of great ships; fog drooping on the gunwales of barges and small boats.

Fog in the eyes and throats of ancient Greenwich pensioners, wheezing by the firesides in their wards; fog in the stem and bowl of the afternoon pipe of the wrathful skipper, down in his close cabin; fog cruelly pinching the toes and fingers of his shivering little 'prentice boy on deck.

Dickens is using semicolons to divide items in lists in long sentences. A semicolon is stronger than a comma, so if complex items are being listed the writer can use commas as subdividers inside the items in the list – although not always. As with commas for lists, you don't need a semicolon if you use 'and', 'but' or 'or' before the final listed item. There is no capital letter after a semicolon unless the word is a proper noun or other word which needs a capital letter in its own right.

For example:

The mouse found nuts, berries and seeds; buried them in cavities in bark, inside the debris of the greenhouse and under rocks; revisited its stashes, ensured the security of the hoards and made final coverings and, during winter dearths, searched them out again.

Exercise 3.8

Use semicolons to divide the items listed in these sentences:

1 I bought oranges, because they are my mother's favourite and she has a bad cold bananas for Peter some fresh dates, which we all like unripe peaches, which will be ready in a few days and a big bag of overripe apples for my horse, who loves them for treats.

2 Our tour of America took us to New England where Dad was fascinated by Boston and its history into California where we didn't like Los Angeles but loved the countryside eastward along the Mexican border eventually to Louisiana and Alabama and included highlights like Charleston in South Carolina.

3 This year Yasmin has already read three books by Charles Dickens, which she says she enjoyed very much most of Daphne du Maurier, including *The Glass Blowers* four modern crime novels biographies of William Pitt and Charles Darwin and quite a lot of poetry.

Spelling and vocabulary

gh- words

The word 'ghoulish' came into English from Arabic in the eighteenth century. In Muslim legend a ghoul was an evil demon thought to eat human bodies – either stolen corpses or children.

A small group of Anglo Saxon-words – such as 'ghost' and 'ghastly' – begin with 'gh-' too. The Anglo-Saxon language, now usually called Old English or OE in dictionaries, was spoken by the people who lived in Britain before it was successfully invaded by William of Normandy in 1066. After the conquest, the Anglo-Saxon language gradually merged with French, which was largely based on Latin.

Other 'gh-' words – 'ghee', 'ghat' and 'gharry' for example – have come into English more recently from Hindi because of Britain's long association with India.

Still more 'gh-' words have come from other sources. We get 'gherkin' from Dutch, 'ghetto' from Italian and 'ghillie' from Scottish Gaelic.

■ An Anglo-Saxon helmet

Exercise 3.9

Use these 'gh-' words in sentences of your own to show that you understand their meaning:

1	gharry	5	ghastly
2	ghetto	6	ghillie
3	ghoulish	7	ghee
4	ghat	8	gherkin

gg words

'Haggard' and 'luggage' are spelt with a double 'g' which is quite common in English.

Exercise 3.10

1 Learn the spellings and meanings (if you need to) of these ten 'gg' words:

aggravate	goggles	priggish
aggressive	laggard	smuggle
arpeggio	niggardliness	toboggan

2 Make a list of ten more words which contain 'gg'.

◯ Functions of language

Breaking the rules

In the extract on page 28, Dickens has written entirely in sentence fragments – part sentences which don't have a formal subject and verb. They are not therefore grammatically 'correct'.

Daphne du Maurier uses this technique (see Chapter 1) but Dickens has taken it further.

Examples:

- Implacable November weather.
- Dogs, indistinguishable in mire.
- Fog everywhere.

This is quite easy to spot in very short sentences, but in this passage longer 'sentences' are fragments too:

- As much mud in the streets, as if the waters had but newly retired from the face of the earth, and it would not be wonderful to meet a Megalosaurus, forty feet long or so, waddling like an elephantine lizard up Holborn Hill.
- Gas looming through the fog in divers places in the streets, much as the sun may, from the spongey fields, be seen to loom by husbandman and ploughboy.

The effect of this is to make Dickens's observations read like notes. (After all, he was a journalist as well as a novelist.) It's a style associated with very personal, impressionistic writing – in diaries for example. And it allows Dickens to start as many sentences as he likes with that plodding, heavy-sounding word 'fog'. If he'd carefully observed the rules of grammar and written 'There was fog everywhere', or 'Fog was everywhere', the impact would have been slower, duller and much less immediate.

One of the differences between poetry and prose is that poems tend to use sentence fragments rather than grammatical sentences. For example:

Face tucked down into a beard, drawn in / Under his hair like a hedgehog's.

No sun – no moon!

This is why Dickens's description of London feels quite poetic as well as vivid.

Exercise 3.11

Copy a section of the *Bleak House* extract, setting it out on the page as if it were a poem. Remember that poems usually begin each new line with a capital letter so you may need to adjust Dickens's capitalisation. Decide how you would have known, if you'd seen your version in a poetry book, that it wasn't written as a poem originally.

Write a paragraph describing a scene you know well using only sentence fragments.

(If you are using a computer, ignore the grammar checker for this exercise.)

There is nothing wrong with breaking grammatical rules, for effect, when you're writing creatively, provided that you understand exactly what you're doing, know why you're doing it and do it with flair – Dickens knew the rules of grammar as well as anyone!

Speaking and listening

1 Learn the Thomas Hood poem by heart and practise reciting it.
2 In groups of about four discuss your experience of, and feelings about, November. Some of the extracts in this chapter regard it rather negatively. Is there anything that you like about November?
3 Imagine you are a television newsreader. Report on the weather in London in an appropriate style for the November day that Dickens describes at the beginning of *Bleak House*. (Imagination is needed here. Of course there was no TV in 1852. Use a modern TV style but take your weather information from the passage.)
4 Organise a class debate on the proposition 'This house thinks that winter is more enjoyable than summer.'
5 Work in a pair. Take it in turns to tell each other about the best book you have read in the last three months.

Extra reading

These books are either connected with the extracts at the beginning of this chapter or they relate in some way to the theme of dark, autumn, November-like days:

● *The Hobbit* by J R R Tolkien (1937)

● Darker plays by Shakespeare such as *King Lear, Othello* and *Hamlet; Shakespeare Stories* (1985) and *Shakespeare Stories II* (1994) by Leon Garfield are a good starting point

● *The Fire-Eaters* by David Almond (2003)

● *The Foreshadowing* by Marcus Sedgwick (2005)

● *Northern Lights* by Philip Pullman (1995)

● *Collected Poems of Ted Hughes*, edited by Paul Keegan (2003)

● *Selected Poems of Thomas Hood*, edited by Joy Flint (1992)

● *A Town like Alice* by Nevil Shute (1950)

- *Bleak House* by Charles Dickens (1852)*

- *Little Dorrit* by Charles Dickens (1857)*

- *Jude the Obscure* by Thomas Hardy (1895)*

- *Heart of Darkness* by Joseph Conrad (1899)*

*Recommended for very keen readers and for those taking scholarship

Progress further

- Find out why fogs – which used to be nicknamed 'pea-soupers' because they were a thick greyish-green and you couldn't see through them – were so much worse in 1852 than they are today. Write a paragraph about this and keep it to refer to.

- Seasonal Affective Disorder (SAD) is a recognised mental health problem and symptoms tend to begin around November. Find out what you can about it. Do you know anyone who suffers from it? What could you – or anyone else – do to help?

- In 2005 the BBC ran a new serialisation of *Bleak House* which many people liked very much. It was issued on DVD (three discs) in February 2006. Watch this (again, if you've seen it before) so that you know the outline story. Then try reading the book.

Villains

A new chaplain

Mr Slope is chaplain, a personal assistant, to the newly appointed Bishop Proudie in nineteenth-century Barchester, a fictional city in the west of England. He is not exactly a hero.

Mr Slope is tall, and not ill made. His feet and hands are large, as has ever been the case with all his family, but he has a broad chest and wide shoulders to carry off these excrescences, and on the whole his figure is good. His countenance, however, is not specially prepossessing. His hair is lank, and of a dull pale reddish
5   hue. It is always formed into three straight lumpy masses, each brushed with admirable precision, and cemented with much grease; two of them adhere closely to the sides of his face, and the other lies at right angles above them. He wears no whiskers, and is always punctiliously shaven. His face is nearly the same colour as his hair, though perhaps a little redder: it is not unlike beef –
10   beef, however, one would say of bad quality. His forehead is capacious and high, but square and heavy, and unpleasantly shining. His mouth is large, though his lips are thin and bloodless; and his big, prominent, pale brown eyes inspire everything except confidence. His nose, however, is his redeeming feature: it is pronounced, straight, and well-formed; though I myself should have liked it
15   better did it not possess a somewhat spongy, porous appearance, as though it had been cleverly formed out of a red coloured cork.

I never could endure to shake hands with Mr Slope. A cold, clammy perspiration always exudes from him, the small drops are even seen standing on his brow, and his friendly grasp is unpleasant.

20   Such is Mr Slope – such is the man who has suddenly fallen into the midst of Barchester Close, and is destined there to assume the station which had hitherto been filled by the son of the late bishop. Think, oh, my meditative reader, what an associate we have here for those comfortable prebendaries, those gentlemanlike clerical doctors, those happy, well-used, well-fed minor
25   canons, who have grown into existence at Barchester under the kindly wings of Bishop Grantly!

But not as mere associate for these does Mr Slope travel down to Barchester
with the bishop and his wife. He intends to be, if not their master, at least the
chief among them. He intends to lead, and to have followers; he intends to hold
30   the purse strings of the diocese, and draw around him an obedient herd of his
poor and hungry brethren.

From Barchester Towers by Anthony Trollope (1857)

Exercise 4.1

Read the extract from *Barchester Towers* and answer the following questions:

1 Summarise Mr Slope's appearance in your own words.

2 What is the name of the previous bishop and what can you deduce about the
attitude of Barchester clergy to him?

3 Who had been chaplain to the previous bishop?

4 Give other words or phrases for (a) excrescences (line 3), (b) punctiliously
(line 8), (c) capacious (line 10) and (d) prebendaries (line 23).

5 What do you learn about Mr Slope's attitude to his new job from this
passage? Use quotations from the passage to support your ideas.

6 What impression does the author want the reader to have of Mr Slope?

'My Last Duchess'

This poem, set in sixteenth-century Italy, was written in 1842.

That's my last duchess painted on the wall,
Looking as if she were alive. I call
That piece a wonder, now: Frà Pandolf's hands
Worked busily a day, and there she stands.
5 Will't please you sit and look at her? I said
'Frà Pandolf' by design, for never read
Strangers like you that pictured countenance,
The depth and passion of its earnest glance,
But to myself they turned (since none puts by
10 The curtain I have drawn for you, but I)
And seemed as they would ask me, if they durst,
How such a glance came there; so, not the first
Are you to turn and ask thus. Sir, 'twas not
Her husband's presence only, called that spot

15 Of joy into the Duchess' cheek: perhaps
    Frà Pandolf chanced to say, 'Her mantle laps
    Over my lady's wrist too much,' or 'Paint
    Must never hope to reproduce the faint
    Half-flush that dies along her throat': such stuff
20 Was courtesy, she thought, and cause enough
    For calling up that spot of joy. She had
    A heart – how shall I say? – too soon made glad,
    Too easily impressed; she liked whate'er
    She looked on, and her looks went everywhere.
25 Sir, 'twas all one! My favour at her breast,
    The dropping of the daylight in the West,
    The bough of cherries some officious fool
    Broke in the orchard for her, the white mule
    She rode with round the terrace – all and each
30 Would draw from her alike the approving speech,
    Or blush, at least. She thanked men – good! but thanked
    Somehow – I know not how – as she ranked
    My gift of a nine-hundred-years-old name
    With anybody's gift. Who'd stoop to blame
35 This sort of trifling? Even had you skill
    In speech – (which I have not) – to make your will
    Quite clear to such an one, and say, 'Just this
    Or that in you disgusts me; here you miss,
    Or there exceed the mark' – and if she let
40 Herself be lessoned so, nor plainly set
    Her wits to yours, forsooth, and made excuse,
    – E'en then would be some stooping; and I choose
    Never to stoop. Oh sir, she smiled, no doubt,
    Whene'er I passed her; but who passed without
45 Much the same smile? This grew; I gave commands;
    Then all smiles stopped together. There she stands
    As if alive. Will't please you rise? We'll meet
    The company below, then. I repeat
    The Count your master's known munificence
50 Is ample warrant that no just pretence
    Of mine for dowry will be disallowed;
    Though his fair daughter's self, as I avowed
    At starting, is my object. Nay, we'll go
    Together down sir. Notice Neptune, though,
55 Taming a sea-horse, thought a rarity,
    Which Claus of Innsbruck cast in bronze for me!

Robert Browning (1842)

Exercise 4.2

Read the poem 'My Last Duchess' and answer the following questions:

1 Who is the narrator of the poem?

2 Whom is the narrator addressing and what is he negotiating for?

3 What has happened to 'my last duchess' and why?

4 Choose and list three or four words or phrases which emphasise the sinister power of the narrator.

5 Why does the speaker mention the sculpture of Neptune at the end?

6 What does rhyme contribute to this poem? Quote from the poem to support your answer.

A review of *Sweeney Todd* at Chichester Festival Theatre

It has long seemed to me that Stephen Sondheim's *Sweeney Todd* is the last of the truly great classic American musicals, right up there with *Guys and Dolls*, *West Side Story*
5   and *My Fair Lady*.

To judge by the ecstatic response that greeted Jonathan Kent's new production which opened last night in Chichester, audiences evidently agree. But though there
10   are undoubtedly many moments here that achieve the right mixture of nervous laughter and spine-tingling terror this strikes me as a production that doesn't quite do justice to a masterpiece.

15   It's perhaps a sign that a show has acquired classic status when a director feels free to start mucking about with it – and Kent does just that. For reasons that escape me he has set the action in what appears to be the 1930s, though the story of the demon barber of Fleet Street, who slits the throats of his customers to furnish the raw materials of the famous pies served in Mrs Lovett's shop
20   beneath, is firmly set in the Victorian era, and inspired by Dickens, penny dreadfuls and 19th century melodrama. Updating it seems merely perverse.

Perhaps Kent's idea was to make the piece seem more 'relevant' by reminding us of the great slump of the 1930s as our economy goes down the plughole yet again, but I do wish he had left well alone.

25   I was also less than persuaded by Michael Ball's performance in the title role. With his pale plump face, goatee beard and lank dark forelock of hair, he certainly looks sinister. But he also looks like David Brent in *The Office*, and his voice doesn't always rise to either the vocal or the dramatic challenges of the role. He tries hard, and certainly dispels the cosy image of his Radio 2

30   programme, but he never quite penetrates the dark rancorous heart of Sweeney.

I have no reservations at all however about Imelda Staunton as the kind and cosy Mrs Lovett who hits on the devilish plan of turning Sweeney's victims into pie fillings and her customers into inadvertent cannibals. There is a wonderful comic zest in her performance and she gets superb value from one of the

35   show's greatest songs, the irresistibly inventive 'A Little Priest' in which she contemplates the ingredients of her pies in such wonderful Sondheim lyrics as 'we have shepherd's pie peppered with actual shepherd on top'.

And her tender, lovelorn yearning for the psychopathic barber somehow proves more poignant and more moving than Sweeney's mountainous sense of

40   injustice and love for his own lost daughter Johanna, feebly played and sung by Lucy May Barker.

The wonderful score, however, with its doomy organ, shrieking industrial sirens and nerve-fraying brass is superbly played and though this is far from being the greatest *Sweeney Todd* I have seen, the musical's mixture of darkness and wit

45   remains as damnably addictive as ever.

From an article written by Charles Spencer and published in the
Daily Telegraph (2011)

Exercise 4.3

Read the review of *Sweeney Todd* and answer the following questions:

1 Who directed this production?

2 Which city was it staged in?

3 Choose three words from the passage which remind you that this show tells the story of a horrifying villain.

4 Explain in your own words the two things which critic Charles Spencer disliked most about this production.

5 What do you learn from Charles Spencer's review about the character Mrs Lovett?

6 What does Spencer admire about Imelda Staunton's performance? Use quotations from the passage in your answer.

Writing practice   Exercise 4.4

1 Imagine you are the Count's daughter who is to be married to the Duke in Browning's poem. Write an entry for your diary describing your first meeting with the man your father has decided you will marry.

2 Write a story entitled 'Not exactly a hero'.

3 You are the daughter or son of a clergyman in Barchester. Mr Slope comes to tea and it is the first time you have met him. Write your impressions. Use your imagination to add to the information in the passage.

4 Write an essay about 'My Last Duchess'. Mention the story that the poem tells, how it is told and the poet's choice of language. Make sure you comment in detail on the effect of some of Browning's words and phrases. You can use some of your answers to Exercise 4.2 as a starting point and also the notes in the 'Functions of language' section on page 52.

5 Write in any way you wish about villains or people who aren't what they seem.

Did you know?

These facts relate to the writers or topics featured in this chapter:

- The word 'villain' originally meant an agricultural worker (a 'villein') but gradually changed to mean a wicked or malevolent person.

- As well as being a prolific novelist, Anthony Trollope was a senior Post Office official and inventor of the pillar box.

- Robert Browning wrote the famous children's poem 'The Pied Piper of Hamelin'.

- The Sweeney Todd story – or legend – has been filmed and staged many times, including the 2007 film starring Johnny Depp and Helena Bonham Carter.

■ A statue of the Pied Piper of Hamelin in Hamelin

Exercise 4.5

Research and note three separate facts to add to the list above. They should relate to villains or to the writers and other topics touched on in this chapter. You should be able to summarise each of your facts in a single sentence.

Grammar and punctuation

Anticipatory phrases

Look at the phrases which open these sentences:

> **One of the only truly classic American musicals**, *Sweeney Todd*, opened at Chichester Festival Theatre in October 2011.

> **Written in the mid-nineteenth century**, Robert Browning's poem tells a sixteenth-century story.

Each is an **anticipatory phrase**. That means that it looks ahead to something which is yet to come in the sentence. Unless something is added the phrase would be meaningless.

The phrase 'One of the only truly classic American musicals' relates to '*Sweeney Todd*' which comes next. The phrase 'written in the mid-nineteenth century' relates to 'Robert Browning's poem'. In both cases the opening phrase anticipates the subject of the sentence.

This is a neat, useful and elegant device in writing because it helps to vary sentence shape and means that fewer sentences repetitively begin with the subject. It can enable a point to be well made in fewer words too.

But it is easy to get it wrong. In English, word order affects meaning. It is important that the subject which the phrase is referring to comes immediately after the anticipatory phrase, otherwise the sentence makes no sense or means something other than the writer intends.

For example:

- One of the only truly classic American musicals, Spencer finds it damnably addictive. (Spencer is not a musical.)
- Written in the nineteenth century, Robert Browning wrote his poem in Florence. (Robert Browning was not written in the nineteenth century.)

Exercise 4.6

Look carefully at these sentences. Some are correct and some are not. Correct (or alter so that they make sense) the ones which are wrong. You may need to change words as well as word order:

1 Always tasty at Pizza Express, I enjoyed lunch.

2 A part-time novelist, Anthony Trollope also worked for the Post Office.

3 Presented many times in different forms, the Sweeney Todd story is very compelling.

4 Her voice very dramatic, the class listened while Fiona read her poem.

5 Falling on 14 February, lovers the world over celebrate St Valentine's Day.

6 Inspired by Robert Browning, a poem a day was Andrew's goal.

Revision of apostrophes for possessive plurals

Remember that in English an apostrophe followed by 's' is used to show possession. The apostrophe and 's' come immediately after the word that is possessing (e.g. 'Paul's friend', 'my sister's dog'). If the possessor is plural, the rule is the same except that we do not add 's' after the apostrophe if the plural possessor already ends in '-s' (which of course it normally does). Thus:

- girls' books (books belonging to several girls)
- ladies' shoes (shoes belonging to more than one lady)
- actresses' scripts (scripts belonging to several actresses)
- foxes' lairs (lairs belonging to several foxes).

Note, however, that if the plural possessor does not end in '-s', add the apostrophe and 's' as normal. Thus:

- men's shoes (shoes belonging to more than one man)
- geese's feathers (feathers belonging to more than one goose).

Exercise 4.7

1 Write these words as plural possessives:

(a) baby   (f) teacher   (k) army
(b) princess   (g) headmistress   (l) author
(c) ibex   (h) bush   (m) country
(d) church   (i) scientist   (n) grandmother
(e) fairy   (j) musician   (o) granny

2 Now put each one of these plural possessives into a sentence of your own.

Spelling and vocabulary

Heteronyms
Look at these sentences:

Browning makes his Duke refuse to stoop.

Perhaps Mrs Lovett puts her scraps out with the refuse.

Mr Slope is keen to present his views to everyone he meets in Barchester.

If Mr Slope visits a lady he usually takes a little present with him.

'Refuse' and 'refuse' look identical when written so we have to deduce what they mean from their context. In speech they sound different because we stress them differently.

If we mean to refuse to do something we say 'refuse'. If we mean rubbish we say 'refuse'. 'Present' and 'present' are another example.

These pairs of words are called **heteronyms**.

Heteronyms are quite common in English because it is a stressed language.

You can change the meaning or function of a word by stressing different parts of it too.

For example:

● pro*duce* and sub*ject* are verbs
● *pro*duce and *sub*ject are nouns.

Sometimes we move the stress when we add prefixes and suffixes to words too. For example, we say:

● *illu*strate but illu*stra*tion
● *stra*tegy but stra*te*gic
● *mem*ory but me*mor*ial
● ap*pear* but *dis*appear.

This is an aspect of English that many people learning it as an acquired language find very difficult. For those of us who grew up speaking and hearing English it usually comes instinctively, but you need to be aware of the tricks the language is playing.

Exercise 4.8

Write two sentences to illustrate the use of each of the following heteronyms:

1 invalid

2 minute

3 second

4 collect

5 contract

6 digest

7 viola

8 console

9 rejoin

10 process

Exercise 4.9

Write sentences using the following words. The stressed syllable is highlighted to help you:

1 fre*quent* (verb)
2 *con*vict (noun)
3 *reb*el (noun)
4 con*test* (verb)
5 ab*sent* (verb)
6 *con*duct (noun)

The silent p

Some words in English begin with a 'p-' which is not pronounced. They come from Greek and they just have to be learnt. For example, 'psychiatrist' comes from the Greek words *psyche*, which means 'mind', and *iatros*, which means 'doctor'.

Study the following list of Greek words which will help with the next exercise:

psōra	an itchy disease
ptōchos	beggarly, poor
pseudōs	false, untrue
psalmos	a song sung to a stringed instrument
pteris	a feathery fern
pneuma	wind, air
pneumōn	lungs
pteron	feather
ptosis	falling

Exercise 4.10

1 Link these definitions with the right meanings on page 52:

air-filled (e.g. a tyre)	serious lung disease
extinct flying reptile	drooping of upper eye lid
poetic prayer, often sung	skin disease
doctor who treats mental illness	false
study of ferns	government by the poor

psoriasis	pteridology
ptochocracy	psychiatrist
ptosis	pneumonia
pseudo	pterodactyl
psalm	pneumatic

2 Now learn the spellings and meanings of these ten words if you don't already know them.

3 List as many different silent 'p' words as you can, using a dictionary to help you. Then make sure you know the meanings and spellings of all the words on your list.

The silent m

If you use 'Never Eat Shredded Wheat' to remember the points of the compass or BIDMAS (Brackets, Index numbers, Divide, Multiply, Add, Subtract) to help remember the order in which maths calculations should be tackled, you are using a **mnemonic** or memory aid. The 'm-' is silent and mnemonic is a very unusual word. Make sure you can spell it. We get the word from **Mnemosyne** who was the goddess of memory in Ancient Greek mythology.

■ *Parnassius mnemosyne* is the Latin name of this species of butterfly, also called Clouded Apollo

Functions of language

Spelling out a subtext

Anthony Trollope's Mr Slope is very unappealing to look at and the reader understands that he isn't very nice to know either. But Trollope doesn't tell you any of this directly. He implies it.

In 'My Last Duchess', Browning is presenting a monologue in verse. The speaker is a ruthless murderer. But, like Trollope, Browning makes his meaning clear by implication rather than by what is actually said.

Conveying ideas by implication rather than by stating them outright is known as **subtext**. Think of it as an underlying message. Playwrights use it in drama when characters don't say what they actually mean but the audience knows what is going on in their minds because of gesture and tone. Novelists and poets do something similar and the term has been borrowed from drama to describe it.

Trollope:

- praises Mr Slope sparingly to suggest that he's being very fair (his nose and his figure)
- uses a lot of negatives to tone down his comments rather than choosing the vocabulary of obvious dislike ('not ill made', 'no whiskers', 'not specially prepossessing')
- chooses humorous imagery expressed with pretend seriousness (bad beef, red cork)
- repeats for emphasis ('intends')
- addresses the reader directly as if we and he are friends sharing a confidential chat ('oh, my meditative reader', 'I never could').

Browning:

- makes the Duke speak very politely and formally ('Will't please you rise?')
- ensures that the Duke is very fluent and convincing – obviously in charge
- gives the Duke very simple vocabulary so that there can be no misunderstanding ('She had / A heart – how shall I say? – too soon made glad')
- never uses direct words like kill, destroy or murder
- conveys power obliquely ('My gift of a nine-hundred-years-old name')
- has the Duke speak chillingly ('There she stands / As if alive').

Exercise 4.11

Re-read the extract from *Barchester Towers*. Write a short summary of Trollope's subtext. What, in plain, blunt language, is he trying to tell us about Mr Slope?

Exercise 4.12

Re-read 'My Last Duchess'. Summarise in a paragraph exactly what the Duke is telling the visitor. Be as direct as you can.

◯ Speaking and listening

1 Read one of the books listed in the next section. Tell a partner about the book, doing your utmost to persuade him or her to read it too.
2 Prepare a reading of the description of Mr Slope. Make it as lively and interesting as you can, remembering to communicate what you think the author really feels.
3 Work in a small group to discuss 'My Last Duchess'. Ensure that the points each person makes relate to the words of the poem. Decide how much you like the poem as a piece of writing and why.

4 Use your work in task 3 as the basis for a prepared reading of the poem to share with other groups.

5 Work in a pair. One of you is Mr Slope. The other is a lady he is visiting in Barchester. It is the first time he has called. Role-play the conversation.

6 Prepare a short talk for the class about a villain either from history or from fiction.

Extra reading

These books either relate to the extracts at the beginning of this chapter or they include people or situations which aren't quite what they seem:

- *Envy* by Gregg Olsen (2011)
- *The Shell House* by Linda Newbery (2002)
- *Scarecrows* by Robert Westall (1981)
- *Postcards from No Man's Land* by Aidan Chambers (1999)
- *The Oxford Book of Villains*, edited by John Mortimer (1992)
- *The Poems of Robert Browning* (1994)
- *Hester's Story* by Adèle Geras (2005)
- *Nineteen Eighty-Four* by George Orwell (1948)
- *Never Let Me Go* by Kazuo Ishiguro (2005)*
- *Barchester Towers* by Anthony Trollope (1857)*
- *The Warden* by Anthony Trollope (1855)*

*Recommended for very keen readers and for those taking scholarship

Progress further

- In the 1980s the BBC serialised *Barchester Towers* and another book in the same series by Anthony Trollope, *The Warden*. Alan Rickman is excellent as Mr Slope. Titled *The Barchester Chronicle*, it is available on DVD. Watch it so that you know the outline story. Then try reading the books.

- Robert Browning (1812–1889) married another poet Elizabeth Barrett (1806–1861), known after their wedding in 1846 as Elizabeth Barrett Browning. The story of their courtship and marriage is pretty remarkable. Find out about their lives and read some (more) of the poetry they each wrote.

- Listen to a recording of Stephen Sondheim's *Sweeney Todd*. Work out what you think about his music and enjoy Mrs Lovett's 'A Little Priest' song!

Beauty

Cleopatra

This is Sir Thomas North's 1579 translation of part of *Lives* by Plutarch, a Greek biographer who lived between approximately 50 and 120 AD. It describes Cleopatra setting out to meet Mark Antony.

> She disdained to set forward otherwise but to take her barge in the river of Cydnus, the poop whereof was of gold, the sails of purple, and the oars of silver, which kept stroke in rowing after the sound of the music of flutes, howboys, citherns, viols and other such instruments as they played upon the barge. And now for the person
> 5 herself: she was laid under a pavilion of cloth of gold of tissue, apparelled and attired like the goddess Venus commonly drawn in picture; and hard by her, on either hand of her, pretty fair boys apparelled as painters do set forth god Cupid, with little fans in their hands, with which they fanned wind upon her.

From *Lives* by Thomas North (1579)

Here is Shakespeare's version as it appears in his 1607 play *Antony and Cleopatra*.

> The barge she sat in, like a burnished throne
> Burned on the water. The poop was beaten gold;
> Purple were the sails, and so perfumèd that
> The winds were lovesick with them. The oars were silver,
> 5 Which to the tune of flutes kept stroke, and made
> The water which they beat to follow faster,

As amorous of their strokes. For her own person,
It beggared all description: she did lie
In her pavilion – cloth of gold, of tissue –
10 O'erpicturing that Venus where we see
The fancy outwork nature. On each side her
Stood pretty dimpled boys, like smiling Cupids,
With divers-coloured fans, whose wind did seem
To glow the delicate cheeks which they did cool,
15 And what they undid did.

From *Antony and Cleopatra* by William Shakespeare (1607)

Exercise 5.1

Read the above extracts from the translation by Sir Thomas North and
Shakespeare's *Antony and Cleopatra* and answer the following questions:

1 What is the most obvious difference between these two pieces of writing?

2 Which river was Cleopatra's barge sailing on?

3 How was the barge driven?

4 What has Shakespeare taken directly from Plutarch, his source, and what has
   he added? Quote from both passages in support of your answer.

5 From Shakespeare's lines explain the meaning of (a) 'It beggared all
   description' (line 8) and (b) 'And what they undid did' (line 15).

6 Which of these two descriptions in the extracts do you prefer and why?

'The Wild Swans at Coole'

The trees are in their autumn beauty,
The woodland paths are dry,
Under the October twilight the water
Mirrors a still sky;
5 Upon the brimming water among the stones
Are nine-and-fifty swans.

The nineteenth autumn has come upon me
Since I first made my count;
I saw, before I had well finished,
10 All suddenly mount

And scatter wheeling in great broken rings
Upon their clamorous wings.

I have looked upon these brilliant creatures,
And now my heart is sore.
15　All's changed since I, hearing at twilight,
The first time on this shore,
The bell-beat of their wings above my head,
Trod with a lighter tread.

Unwearied still, lover by lover,
20　They paddle in the cold
Companionable streams or climb the air;
Their hearts have not grown old;
Passion or conquest, wander where they will,
Attend upon them still.

25　But now they drift on the still water,
Mysterious, beautiful;
Among what rushes will they build,
By what lake's edge or pool
Delight men's eyes when I wake some day
30　To find they have flown away?

W B Yeats (1917)

Exercise 5.2

Read the poem 'The Wild Swans at Coole' and answer the following questions:

1　For how long has the narrator been observing the swans?

2　What time of year and what time of day is it?

3　How many birds are there?

4　Which words and phrases describe the sound of the swans?

5　In what way does he find them beautiful?

6　What is the mood of the poem? Consider the whole poem in your response.

Hair today and gone tomorrow

All cities have lots of them. Like mushrooms they spring up when no one's looking. Once they were simply called hairdressers or barbers but today they use pretentious vocabulary borrowed from other professions and life styles. 'Treatments' are recommended in 'salons' by 'hair consultants', 'designers' or 'stylists'.

5   In their expensively fitted-out shops, punningly named things like 'Prime Cuts', 'Hair and Now' or 'Head Line', city hairdressers are getting above themselves in a big way. Their premises are deliberately made to look like up-market clinics (without being clinical of course) with the staff in white uniforms, faintly reminiscent of nurses. Hairdressers, let it not be forgotten, are the descendants of servants – ladies' maids
10   and the like. They are not related to professions like medicine.

And what happens when you get inside these hairdressers' shops? The client – they have yet to call the customers 'patients' but it won't be long – submits, at considerable expense, to guidance and advice from a *soi-disant* expert about her hair. The hair is in 'poor condition'. It is probably 'damaged'. By what? By perm
15   lotions, neutralisers, colouring agents and other of the favourite witches' brew of chemicals which are the hairdresser's stock-in-trade. Not to mention the plethora of gels, mousses, conditioners, protein rinses and so on – all, of course, at extra cost. Hair driers, rollers, heated tongs don't do the hair much good either.

The effrontery of the hypocrisy is astonishing. As you sit and listen to all
20   this sanctimonious tripe you are probably watching in the mirror another customer as she voluntarily offers her head for some sort of chemical bath or worse. Not a shred of reluctance or reservation about 'damage' from the practitioner at this stage. It provides self-perpetuating employment for her colleagues in the future, I suppose.

25   What hair actually needs for normal healthy maintenance is periodic washing with a minimum amount of shampoo, maybe a smear of conditioner and then to be allowed to dry naturally. And you don't need to be any kind
30   of expert, self-styled or otherwise, to know that.

The trouble is, if everyone took the common sense line, there'd be thousands
35   of redundant hairdressers and product and equipment manufacturers. It's big business. And what about

those who dignify their profession with a quasi-scientific title such as 'trichology'
40 and write learned advice in women's magazines?

After thirty years of submission to the conning abuses of 'good' hairdressers, especially the sort who congregate in city centres and never charge less than £25 per visit, I am now shot of their less than benign attentions.

I have declared unilateral independence by growing my hair long. I wash it,
45 brush it and wear it twisted in a bun on the top of my head exactly as I did as a teenager, although it's a bit greyer these days. A minor but satisfying blow for autonomy.

Susan Elkin (1993)

Exercise 5.3

Read the article by Susan Elkin and answer the following questions:

1 Give another word or phrase for (a) pretentious (line 3), (b) reminiscent (line 8), (c) effrontery (line 19) and (d) autonomy (line 47).

2 Find words in the passage which mean (a) self-styled and (b) academic-sounding.

3 What damages hair, in the writer's opinion?

4 Explain in your own words why the writer thinks that the hairdressing profession is hypocritical.

5 Summarise the writer's own recommendations for healthy hair.

6 Why does the writer now do without hairdressers?

7 Identify and comment on four 'value judgement' words or phrases in this passage – the ones which indicate the writer's own views.

Writing practice Exercise 5.4

1 The article about hairdressers is intended for adults. Write a warning leaflet for teenagers about the dangers of some form of 'beauty treatment'.

2 Imagine you are one of the boys fanning Cleopatra. Write what you tell a friend that evening when you have finished work.

3 Write an essay comparing Shakespeare's description of Cleopatra's barge with the source he took it from. Comment in detail on Shakespeare's words and style. (You can use some of the work you did in Exercise 5.1 to help you.)

4 Write a poem or an imaginative prose account of something you have seen or witnessed which struck you as beautiful.

5 Research and write a factual article about swans. Include what makes them different from other birds, their food, habitat, breeding and behaviour.

6 'Beauty is only skin deep.' How far do you agree or disagree? Write an essay setting out your views. Use examples to support your arguments.

7 Write about beauty in any way you wish.

Did you know?

These facts relate to the writers or topics featured in this chapter:

- In the seventeenth century obese women were regarded as beautiful, which is why the artist Peter Paul Rubens featured so many large ladies in his paintings.

- William Shakespeare's father, John, was a Stratford-upon-Avon tradesman who could neither read nor write.

- William Butler Yeats, probably the most famous Irish poet of all time, died in 1939.

- The Hairdressing Council was founded in 1964 to establish and maintain a list of qualified, professional hairdressers.

Exercise 5.5

Research and note three separate facts to add to the list above. They should relate to beauty or to the writers and other topics touched on in this chapter. You should be able to summarise each of your facts in a single sentence.

Grammar and punctuation

Direct and indirect speech

If we quote exactly what someone says in, for example, a story or a newspaper article, that is **direct speech**.

For example:

> 'Hair driers, rollers, heated tongs don't do the hair much good,' says Susan Elkin.

Susan Elkin's exact words are quoted verbatim (word for word). They therefore have to be enclosed in inverted commas and need some other punctuation mark – in this case a comma – at the end.

Compare this example from a newspaper report:

> Dr Nigel Carter, the chief executive of the British Dental Health Foundation, says that even whitening toothpastes, which are largely ineffective in lightening teeth, should not be used more than twice a day, as they tend to be abrasive, and overuse may damage the surface enamel of teeth.

The journalist who interviewed Dr Carter is summarising in her own words what he has said. This is called indirect or reported speech and needs no inverted commas. It often needs a link word such as 'that' after the speech verb – in this case 'says' – because the words spoken are not the direct object of the verb.

Sometimes verbs need to be put in a different tense too.

For example:

> Susan Elkin said 'I do not visit hairdressers any more.'

> Susan Elkin said that she did not visit hairdressers any more.

> Mr Harvey-Maynard stated, 'I believe you've seen enough of this, class?'

> Mr Harvey-Maynard stated that he believed the class had seen enough of this.

Exercise 5.6

The following sentences all use direct speech. Rewrite them in indirect speech. You will need to change word order and/or add or replace words. Make sure you punctuate them correctly. Remember indirect speech is the writer summarising what someone else has said.

1. 'I first saw *Antony and Cleopatra* at Chichester Festival Theatre in 1979,' our English teacher told us.

2. 'Mysterious, beautiful,' wrote Yeats of the swans at Coole.

3. 'A thing of beauty is a joy for ever,' wrote poet John Keats.

4. The Queen often begins her speeches with the words 'My husband and I'.

5. 'Lead on!' said the explorer to his companion.

6. My grandmother said, 'I have just read *Bleak House*.'

Exercise 5.7

Rewrite these sentences using direct speech. You will need to use inverted commas and other punctuation.

1 The actor told his friends that he had enjoyed playing Antony.

2 Our headmaster hopes that the new building will be finished by the beginning of next term.

3 According to Dr Carter, it is dangerous to whiten your teeth too often.

4 Mum had a headache so Dad asked us to be as quiet as we could.

5 Aunty Usha told us that she had made plans to spend Christmas in Papua New Guinea this year.

6 Temi explained that she wanted to go to Granny's via the supermarket in order to buy her some chocolates.

Hyphens in adjectival phrases

Writers often use hyphens as links when they want to use a whole idea or an expression as if it were a single adjective:

- whiter-than-white
- glow-in-the-dark
- over-the-counter

This is quite a creative way of using language. It enables the writer to come up with new, concise ways of describing things.

Exercise 5.8

Turn the following expressions into hyphen-linked adjectives and use them in sentences of your own:

1 black as night

2 one size fits all

3 open for business

4 dry as dust

5 fed up with school

○ Spelling and vocabulary

The origins of names

Shakespeare was a playwright. **'Wright'** is a thousand-year-old word from Old English (the language spoken in England before the Norman Conquest in 1066). It means 'a maker'.

So Shakespeare was a maker of plays. **Cartwrights** and **wheelwrights** made carts and wheels, respectively.

The names of many old crafts are still alive in English today – as surnames. **Baker**, **Brewer**, **Shepherd** and **Fisher** are all very common names, for example. If you have such a name it means that at some point – probably hundreds of years ago – one of your ancestors was known in his community by the job he did and that became the family name.

It is very obvious what names like **Butcher**, **Farmer** and **Miller** mean and you can probably make your own, quite long, list of such names. But what about the less obvious ones such as **Parker** or **Chapman**?

Exercise 5.9

Use a general dictionary or a dictionary of names to link the following surnames with their meanings:

Parker	jeweller
Chapman	gamekeeper in a park
Cordwainer	trader
Wainwright	blacksmith
Cooper	supplier of goods for ships
Palmer	barrel maker
Goldsmith	pilgrim home from the Holy Land
Sawyer	leather worker
Chandler	a cutter of wood
Mercer	cart maker
Farrier	cloth merchant

Neologisms

'**Trichologist**' (hair expert) is an example of a newly invented word coined to describe a new idea, person, thing or trend. People – especially journalists – coin new words (neologisms) all the time, often by making a new version of an older word – such as '**shopaholic**' or '**chocoholic**' to describe people who are addicted to shopping or chocolate in the same way as alcoholics are addicted to alcohol.

Others are based on acronyms or near acronyms such as '**nimby**' which stands for 'not in my back yard', and is applied to people who don't mind new building unless it's close to their own homes. Texting has produced neologisms such as **LOL** for 'laugh out loud' or, sometimes, 'lots of love', **BIF** (before I forget) and **HOAS** (hold on a second) among others, although accurate and fast predictive texting may mean that some of these are already dying out.

Some of these neologisms become established and find their way into dictionaries as part of our growing and changing language. Others disappear very quickly.

Exercise 5.10

Find out what the following neologisms mean and use them in sentences of your own:

1 staycation
2 technophobe
3 crowdfund
4 photobomb
5 townscape

6 wordsmith
7 telethon
8 Oxfam
9 Ofsted
10 cyberspace

The sometimes silent n

Autumn is one of a small group of words in which 'm' is followed by a silent 'n'. The 'n', however, *is* pronounced when autumn takes a syllable in its adjectival form: autum**n**al.

Other words which behave in a similar way include:

● condemn (condem**n**ation, condem**n**atory)
● solemn (solem**n**ity).

Exercise 5.11

Put these words into the spaces in the sentences which follow:

autumnal   solemnity   columnist   condemnation   columnar

1 Church services usually have an atmosphere of _____.

2 Jan Moir is a regular _____ for the *Daily Mail*.

3 _____ weather is only to be expected in October.

4 At our school's main entrance is a large _____ area.

5 Because she lied to us all she earned the _____ of almost everyone in the class.

The disappearing u

Shakespeare used the word 'amorous' and Yeats the word 'clamorous' in the extracts in this chapter.

Look carefully at the spellings of these words because the nouns they come from are 'amour' (a French word) and 'clamour'. When they become adjectives they lose a 'u'. In Chapter 4 Charles Spencer uses the word 'rancorous' which behaves in the same way.

Exercise 5.12

1 Write the adjective which comes from these nouns. They all follow the same rule:

(a) vigour

(b) humour

(c) glamour

(d) clamour

(e) rancour

2 Now make sure you know what all these words mean.

Functions of language

Using language polemically

In the article on pages 58–59, Susan Elkin is making an argued case against the hairdressing industry. Although she knows that not everyone would agree, she expresses her views in strong language and does not acknowledge that there could be another equally valid point of view. There is nothing even-handed about this writing.

Such an article is known as a **polemic** – from the Ancient Greek word *polemos*, 'war'. The author is, in a sense, waging war against hairdressers. Someone who writes (or speaks) in this style is called a **polemicist**.

But this article was intended for a magazine so it also has to entertain. That is why Susan Elkin opens her piece with a jokey 'hook' about mushrooms to get the reader's attention and make him/her read on and why she doesn't reveal what she is talking about until the third sentence. It is also why, occasionally, she uses slightly flippant expressions like 'they have yet to call the customers "patients"' and 'blow for autonomy'.

Most of her text is a fairly serious, angry attempt to draw the attention of readers to something they may not have thought about before. It is the sort of article which would make readers react – in agreement or disagreement. So there would probably be published letters about it in the next issue of the magazine.

Susan Elkin:

- uses everyday language ('Hair driers, rollers, heated tongs don't do the hair much good either.')
- uses less common words ('plethora', 'effrontery') when she needs to because she is assuming that her reader is adult and well educated
- directly questions the reader to involve him or her ('And what happens when you get inside these hairdressers' shops?')
- ridicules hairdressers by accusing them of behaving as if they were medical practitioners
- reminds readers that hairdressers are the descendants of servants
- ends with an anecdote about her own hair to establish herself as a real, approachable and sensible person
- uses some contracted forms of words ('don't', 'there'd') to create a conversational tone
- uses personal pronouns ('I', 'you') which give the piece directness.

Exercise 5.13

Write a short polemic for a magazine – two or three paragraphs – expressing angrily your views on something about which you feel, or can pretend to feel, strongly. It could be the decision not to put speed bumps in your street, the attitude of the burger industry to health or anything else you wish. Use the same techniques as Susan Elkin, including words and phrases which carry value judgements.

Speaking and listening

1 Work in a group. Devise an advertising campaign for a tooth whitening product. You could create posters, a script for TV or radio or an article for newspapers, magazines, the internet or some other medium – you choose.
2 Work in a group of three. One of you is a hairdresser, one of you agrees with Susan Elkin, and the third is a radio presenter. Rehearse the three-minute conversation you will have on the programme. Perform your work to the rest of the class.

3 Work with a partner. One of you is Enobarbus, the character in *Antony and Cleopatra* who describes Cleopatra on her barge. The other is the person he is speaking to, who must respond appropriately. Work out an updated version, taking it in turns to be Enobarbus.

4 Imagine you are W B Yeats's narrator. You have just seen the swans again this year. Think about what you would say to a friend about this. Write out your thoughts in prose using your own words. Include how you felt as well as what you saw and heard. You can invent further details of your own if you want to go beyond what is in the poem. Then share your piece with someone else in your class.

Extra reading

These books feature beauty or beautiful people:

- *Olivia's First Term* by Lyn Gardner (2011)
- *Ivy* by Julie Hearn (2006)
- *Love, Aubrey* by Suzanne LaFleur (2009)
- *The White Darkness* by Geraldine McCaughrean (2005)
- *Antony and Cleopatra* by William Shakespeare (Leon Garfield's lively retelling in *Shakespeare Stories II* is useful.)
- Any of the many versions of the traditional story of Beauty and the Beast, the Arthurian legend of 'The Loathly Damsel' and the Greek legend of Narcissus
- *Troy* by Adèle Geras (2000)
- *Sisterland* by Linda Newbery (2003)
- Poems by W B Yeats; collections of Yeats's poetry are in many anthologies
- *The Picture of Dorian Grey* by Oscar Wilde (1890)
- *Death in Venice* by Thomas Mann (1912)*

*Recommended for very keen readers and for those taking scholarship

Progress further

- Find and read the poems 'Storm in the Black Forest' by D H Lawrence and 'Pied Beauty' by Gerard Manley Hopkins. If you like them, use them as a starting point for a personal collection of poems about beauty.

- Look at some art books containing figure paintings from previous centuries or find them on the internet. Look at the work of, for example, Michelangelo, Rubens, Titian, Gainsborough and Dante Gabriel Rossetti. Or better still visit a gallery. Then look at some modern magazines which have photographs of fashion models and others. In what ways have ideas about beauty – especially for women – changed? Why do you think this is? You could prepare an illustrated presentation about this for the rest of the class.

■ The portrait 'St Cecilia' by Paul Rubens

5 Beauty

68

6 Risk, adventure and exploration

Roof climbing

The narrator of Barbara Vine's novel *Grasshopper* describes a very risky hobby – really an obsession – in which she and a group of friends are regularly involved.

The most difficult kinds of roof to walk on are those on buildings put up in the past 100 years. These roofs are usually tiled, either with peg tiles or pantiles, and they slope steeply. It is as if architects like Lutyens and Mackintosh and Voysey only realised in the twentieth century that it rains a lot here and steep slopes on
5   roofs provide better drainage. The best kinds are shallow and made of slates, preferably with a stone coping or low wall at the edge, designed to hide from view the fact that the roof slopes at all. The more ornamentation on a roof the better, the more gables, belvederes, single chimney stacks and mansarding, the easier it is to climb. Single detached houses are useless to the serious climber.
10 Standing alone as they do, no matter how shallow their roofs, no matter how many footholds the tops of their dormer windows, their pediments and parapet rails provide, they remain islands. The open air, the gap between them and the house next door, which may be several or many feet, is the sea which divides them from the continent. Climbers need terraces, each house joined to the one
15 next door and preferably not divided from it at roof level by a stack that is a barrier to their progress, a high wall spanning the breadth of the roof and carrying a dozen closely set chimney pots or cowls.

The experienced climber despises television aerials and dishes as aids to balance keeping. He treads fast and light-footed on tile and coping and window ledge.
20 He understands that the first big mistake the climber makes is to dislodge a slate and set it clattering down to ricochet off the coping and crash on the ground. He holds on only to that which is firm and steady, avoiding 100-year-old chimney pots, drainpipes and flimsy plaster mouldings. The best climbers are light in weight and supple.

25 Most roof sounds pass unheard by the householder who knows it's impossible anyone is walking in the sky up above her head. What she hears must be the wind, the rustling and rasping of tree branches. Or a cat may be up there. She has seen a cat on these roofs. At the veterinary practice in St John's Wood they tell her that most of the cats they treat are brought in with broken legs. The cat on the roof or
30 balcony sees a butterfly and leaps in pursuit of it into the shining void.

We were like cats but we saw no butterflies. Mostly we went on the roofs after dark. In daylight you had the view, north London laid out below you, Hampstead Heath and Highgate Wood, the heights of Mill Hill, the canal coming out of its tunnels and entering Regent's Park, but by day you might be seen. Not everyone
35   is in her car or stares at the ground when she walks. Once or twice we were seen but nothing came of it. What would you think if you saw three people in blue jeans and dark sweaters up on the roof of mansion flats? That they were workmen putting up an aerial of course, or doing repairs to the guttering.

By night the lights were strung out and spread and scattered below us. No
40   unpolluted sky was ever so starry. But up where we were, above the lights, the darkness was like thin smoke, the clouds and clear spaces above us stained plum-coloured. When I first began I carried a torch and Liv had the inevitable candle until Wim stopped her. We must learn to see in the dark, he said, as he did. He was our teacher, as it might be a ski instructor with a class of novices on the slopes.

45   At my school, on the last day of term, the fourth form traditionally played a game called 'round and round the room'. You had to circle the gym from the main entrance and back without once touching the floor, and you did it by means of wall bars, a horse, a climbing frame and, of course, ropes. People who inadvertently tapped the floor with a toe were disqualified. The winner was the
50   boy or girl to do it in the shortest time. I won it easily in my fourth-form year and got the prize, a tiny silver (silver plate) cat, but unfortunately you can't take A-levels in negotiating gyms. The roofs of Maida Vale became my gym and a lot of other things besides. For a little while.

People would think you mad, or at least very eccentric, if you told them you
55   climbed on roofs. Of course, you seldom do tell anyone because you know what the reaction will be. They don't understand. They want to know why. But you might as well shoot up some heroin or drink brandy or go dancing or climb mountains

or do white-water rafting. They like it or they thought they would like it when they began.

60 It takes a certain kind of person. No one who was afraid of heights would attempt it. No one unfit or unsure on their feet *should* attempt it. It takes a kind of lawlessness, an unconventional spirit. Claustrophobics are good at it. Some, a very few, are geniuses at it. Wim was, we weren't. Liv wasn't, and Jonny, though good, wasn't in Wim's class. For us, it was the freedom we could find nowhere
65 else, but once we had pushed ourselves to the limits of what we could do and experienced it to the full, we wanted it no longer.

From *Grasshopper* by Barbara Vine (2000)

Exercise 6.1

Read the extract from *Grasshopper* and answer the following questions:

1 Which roofs, according to the author, are the best to walk on?

2 Sum up in your own words the qualities a good roof climber needs.

3 Why, according to the narrator, is it unlikely that anyone will report a roof climber for trespass? (You should be able to find two reasons.)

4 Use a dictionary to find the meaning of (a) pantiles (line 2), (b) belvederes (line 8) and (c) mansarding (line 8)?

5 What, according to the narrator, is the attraction of roof climbing? Use quotations from the passage to support your ideas.

'The Lotos-Eaters'

Odysseus and his men are lost on their way home from the Trojan War. In this extract, the Victorian poet Alfred Lord Tennyson describes them landing on a strange island inhabited by people who eat only the fruit of the lotos-plant. The story comes from Book IX of *The Odyssey* by Homer.

'Courage!' he said, and pointed toward the land,
'This mounting wave will roll us shoreward soon.'
In the afternoon they came unto a land
In which it seemed always afternoon.
5 All round the coast the languid air did swoon,
Breathing like one that hath a weary dream.
Full-faced above the valley stood the moon;
And like a downward smoke, the slender stream
Along the cliff to fall and pause did seem.

10   A land of streams! Some, like a downward
       smoke,Slow-dropping veils of thinnest
       lawn, did go;And some thro' wavering
       lights and shadows broke,Rolling a
       slumberous sheet of foam below.
15   They saw the gleaming river seaward
       flow From the inner land: far off, three
       mountain tops,Three silent pinnacles
       of aged snow,Stood sunset-flush'd: and,
       dew'd with showery drops,Up-clomb the
20   shadowy pine above the woven copse.

       The charmed sunset linger'd low adown
       In the red West: thro' mountain clefts the dale
       Was seen far inland, and the yellow down
       Border'd with palm, and many a winding vale
25   And meadow, set with slender galingale;[1]
       A land where all things always seem'd the same!
       And round about the keel the faces pale,
       Dark faces pale against the rosy flame,
       The mild-eyed Lotos-eaters came.

30   Branches they bore of that enchanted stem,
       Laden with flower and fruit, whereof they gave
       To each, but whoso did receive of them,
       And taste, to him the gushing of the wave
       Far far away did seem to mourn and rave
35   On alien shores; and if his fellow spake,
       His voice was thin, as voices from the grave;
       And deep-asleep he seem'd, yet all awake,
       And music in his ears his beating heart did make.

       They sat him on the yellow sand,
40   Between the sun and moon upon the shore;
       And sweet it was to dream of Fatherland,
       Of child, and wife, and slave; but evermore
       Most weary seem'd the sea, weary the oar,
       Weary the wandering fields of barren foam.
45   Then someone said, 'We will return no more,'
       And all at once they sang, 'Our island home
       Is far beyond the wave; we will no longer roam.'

Alfred Lord Tennyson (1832)   [1] A spice similar to ginger

Exercise 6.2

Read 'The Lotos-Eaters' and answer the following questions:

1 Describe the island in your own words.

2 What did the inhabitants of the island give the sailors and what effect did it have on them?

3 Explain the meaning of (a) languid (line 5), (b) alien (line 35) and (c) barren (line 44).

4 Choose and comment on five or six words which Tennyson chooses for their sound and the atmosphere they help to create.

5 Look carefully at the way Tennyson has arranged his stanzas and at the rhyme pattern. What do you think this adds to the poem as a whole?

'Sacked over 'elf and safety, teacher who took two boys of 15 sledging as part of technology lesson'

A teacher was sacked after letting children use his sledge in the snow as part of a lesson because he failed to carry out a risk assessment.

Richard Tremelling, 37, took the racing sledge into school to demonstrate design technology to his class of 15-year-olds.

5 As part of the demonstration, he tested conditions on two snowy slopes himself before deciding they were safe enough for two boys to follow suit.

The boys were unharmed. But Mr Tremelling was sacked from his £40,000-a-year job as head of technology for breaching health and safety rules.

Yesterday he appeared before the General Teaching Council for Wales at the
10 start of a two-day hearing to decide his future.

Campaigners and MPs said the decision to sack him was 'absolutely disgraceful' and 'ludicrous'.

Nick Seaton, chair of the Campaign for Real Education, warned that the 'heavy-handed' punishment 'would only succeed in discouraging good candidates from
15 joining the teaching profession'.

He added: 'I don't think too many people would consider sledging to be dangerous for children of the age of 15, particularly when under the watchful eye of their teacher.

'Mr Tremelling should be commended for thinking outside the box and attempting to make his lesson more interesting for his class by introducing a practical element. That he has lost his job over it is absolutely disgraceful.'

Rosa Fernandes, presenting the case, said: 'Mr Tremelling took the sledge to school without the authorisation of the head.

'He failed to carry out appropriate risk assessments and failed to provide a written risk assessment.

'He didn't ensure pupils were wearing protective headgear and protective clothing.'

Mr Tremelling told the hearing he took the sledge into the 650-pupil Cefn Hengoed Community School in Swansea as a teaching aid to incorporate the weather conditions into a lesson.

He said he discussed the manufacture and use of the sledge with pupils during a revision class.

'A number of pupils stayed behind interested and excited,' he added. 'They wanted to see it in use and, giving it some thought, I agreed.'

The experienced teacher said he conducted a 'mental risk assessment' before sliding down a small slope, covered in two to three inches of snow, on the sledge.

Two of the pupils, aged 15, then volunteered to ride the sledge, one after the other.

Mr Tremelling said: 'I told the first boy to follow the track marks that I'd laid out – which he did in a safe manner.

'I wanted to demonstrate sledge control so I moved to a different slope. I went first – it was a bit fast so I was not happy for the child to go from the top.

'He started from halfway down the slope and completed the turn correctly.

'The whole process took less than ten minutes and I was sure it reinforced their knowledge.'

Tory MP Philip Davies said Mr Tremelling's case was a perfect example of the 'health and safety obsession' in Britain today.

He added: 'What has happened to this teacher is absolutely ludicrous, even in this day and age. The school appears guilty of a ridiculous overreaction.'

Lord Young, the former Cabinet minister and Tory peer, completed a report into the health and safety rules surrounding classrooms and school trips in October.

He recommended introducing a single consent form to cover all activities a child may undertake during their time at a school.

Other recommendations include cutting back a 12-page risk assessment that
55 teachers have to complete before each school trip.

He criticised the 'enormous bureaucracy' which caused many teachers to avoid organising such activities, depriving millions of children of a vital part of their education. All his recommendations are now being implemented.

Mr Tremelling was suspended following the sledge lesson after a snowfall in
60 February 2009. He was dismissed in January last year.

He denies unacceptable
professional conduct and faces
a reprimand on his record,
suspension or being struck off if the
65 allegations are proven.

Mr Tremelling's union, the
NASUWT, declined to comment
while proceedings were ongoing.

The hearing in Cardiff is expected
70 to end today.

From an article written by Andy Dolan and published in
the *Daily Mail* and *Mail Online* (2011)

Exercise 6.3

Read the article by Andy Dolan and answer the following questions:

1 What rule did Mr Tremelling break?

2 What is the name of the school Mr Tremelling worked in and what was his job?

3 He has been sacked from his job but what other penalties could await him?

4 Summarise in your own words exactly what Mr Tremelling did on a snowy day in February 2009.

5 What, according to Philip Davies and Lord Young, is wrong with health and safety rules?

6 Is there anything in this article which suggests that Andy Dolan and his newspaper have a view of their own? If so, what is it? Use close reference to the text to support your answer.

Writing practice — Exercise 6.4

1 Write about any experience you have of an adventurous or 'risky' activity (such as bungee jumping, parachuting, ballooning or anything else that you found exhilarating).

2 Write a story which begins either with someone landing on an unusual island or having a serious accident in a laboratory.

3 Write a poem or prose description of a place known to you which has, for some reason, a very specific atmosphere (for example, Venice during carnival week, your home area on Christmas Day or London in the rain).

4 Imagine that you have spotted a group of young people roof climbing. Write a letter to a newspaper expressing your views. Then write an answer from someone who disagrees with you.

5 Write an essay about Tennyson's 'The Lotos-Eaters'. Using some of the work you have already done in Exercise 6.2 as a starting point, comment on how the poet achieves his effects. Do you like the result? Explain your reasons.

6 Write about risk in any way you wish.

Did you know?

These facts relate to the writers or topics featured in this chapter:

- *Grasshopper* is by Ruth Rendell, who died in 2015. She wrote some of her novels as Barbara Vine.

- Tennyson, who became a close friend of Queen Victoria because both had houses on the Isle of Wight, was Poet Laureate from 1850 until his death in 1892.

- Today's legal approach to risk stems from the Health and Safety at Work Act of 1974, although there have been changes and amendments to it since then.

- Teachers are required to 'assess risk' – usually in writing – for every activity pupils undertake.

- The *Daily Mail* was first published in 1896.

Exercise 6.5

Research and note three separate facts to add to the list on the previous page. They should relate to risk or to the writers and other topics touched on in this chapter. You should be able to summarise each of your facts in a single sentence.

Grammar and punctuation

Direct and indirect questions

'Do you like Ruth Rendell's novels?' asked Mrs Ali in our English lesson. (**direct**)

In English Mrs Ali asked us whether (or not) we liked Ruth Rendell's novels. (**indirect**)

'Has the Health and Safety policy been circulated to all staff yet?' enquired the headmaster. (**direct**)

The headmaster wanted to know if the Health and Safety Policy had yet been circulated to all staff. (**indirect**)

'What sort of locks do you have on your front door?' asked the policeman first. (**direct**)

The policeman's first question was about the locks on our front door. (**indirect**)

Like statements (see pages 60–61), questions can be asked directly or indirectly. The direct form needs speech marks and a question mark and tends to be shorter. It is used a lot in fiction and drama. It seems more chatty and informal.

The indirect form needs no question mark or speech marks. It often needs a conjunction like 'if' or 'whether'. It is used a lot in reports of meetings (the headmaster asked those present for their views) and in everyday conversation when you can't remember someone's exact words so you summarise or paraphrase when you retell the conversation to someone else (Mum wondered aloud why Dad was so late). In indirect questions, as in indirect statements, the tense of the verb sometimes needs to be changed (e.g. 'Why **are** you singing?' – He asked why you **were** singing).

Newspaper reports use both forms – often in the same article – for variety. Remember that there are a number of verbs which can be used for expressing questions in your writing. They include:

asked	questioned	wondered
queried	demanded	enquired

Exercise 6.6

Rewrite these direct questions in an indirect form. You will need to change some words. Be as creative as you wish as long as the meaning remains the same.

1 'Can't you see I'm busy?' my brother said crossly.

2 'Why is so little Italian taught in British schools?' questioned the Italian Ambassador during her visit to our school.

3 Mum asked, 'Have you got a minute to lay the table for supper?'

4 'When was the Battle of Waterloo?' we were asked in history today.

5 'Are you sure it was Alexander Fleming who discovered penicillin and not Marie Curie?' Tom asked.

6 'What's for lunch today?' wondered Ella, as she headed for the menu board.

Exercise 6.7

Rewrite these sentences to include direct questions. Each will need speech marks and a question mark.

1 Our form tutor wondered whether there was a reason for our not being in school uniform.

2 Tariq's enquiry was about the train's departure time.

3 Granny was curious to know which car we had come in.

4 It was the whereabouts of Newcastle which was exciting Chloe.

5 When the school was inspected we were asked how many hours of prep we had to do.

6 The interviewer wanted to know why the Member of Parliament didn't vote.

◯ Spelling and vocabulary

Adjectives which end in '-n' like 'barren' double their 'n' when they take the suffix 'ness' and become nouns. If you speak slowly both 'n' sounds are pronounced too. So:

barren (adjective) + ness = barrenness (noun)

Exercise 6.8

Convert the following adjectives to nouns and use them in sentences of your own:

1 keen

2 drunken

3 open

4 thin

5 even

6 outspoken

Archaisms

Tennyson deliberately used some words and word forms in his poem which were not used in everyday English in 1832 and certainly aren't now. These are known as **archaisms**. He chose them because he wanted his poem to sound as if it came from a much earlier time. Tennyson's archaisms include:

- up-clomb (old past tense of 'to climb' – now 'climbed')
- clefts ('cuts through'; can you think of modern words which still relate to this?)
- whoso ('anyone')
- spake (old past tense of verb 'to speak' – now 'spoke').

Exercise 6.9

Shakespeare's plays were first published in full in 1623, seven years after his death. The King James Bible, which was one of the first editions of the Bible in English, was published in 1611. Both texts are full of archaisms.

Find out what these archaisms from the Bible and Shakespeare once meant:

1 divers (as an adjective)

2 groat

3 multitudes

4 corse

5 fain

6 hie

7 twain

8 verily

9 sirrah

10 chough

Malapropisms

Many people misuse words because they are similar to other words in sound or spelling and so become confused. Such errors are called **malapropisms** because a very funny character named Mrs Malaprop in Richard Brinsley Sheridan's 1775 play *The Rivals* makes these mistakes all the time. For example, she says:

- 'He is the very pineapple of politeness!'
- 'She's as headstrong as an allegory on the banks of the Nile.'

Use each of these pairs of words in two separate sentences to show that you know the difference between them:

1 flout, flaunt

2 plaintiff, plaintive

3 sceptic, septic

4 moral, morale

5 deprecate, depreciate

The suffix -ee

An employee is someone who is employed by an employer. For example, Mr Tremelling was an employee of Cefn Hengoed Community School. The 'ee' suffix is attached to the root verb 'employ' to create a noun which means the person is, in some sense, subjected to the action of that verb. In the same way we get:

- **devotee** (one who is devoted)
- **absentee** (one who has absented him/herself)
- **trainee** (one who is being trained).

New '-ee' words are often made up. Some teachers call the pupils in their tutor group their **tutees**. When people have been vaccinated some doctors call them **vaccinees**.

Exercise 6.11

List as many examples of '-ee' words as you can.

Functions of language

News reporting

Andy Dolan is writing for a newspaper which prides itself on easy-to-read directness. The main purpose of Dolan's article is to give factual information about Mr Tremelling's sacking, disciplinary hearing and the background to it. It is a piece of news reporting which appeared in the *Daily Mail*'s news section – not on its comment or feature pages. Its secondary purpose is to hint that Mr Tremelling is the victim of injustice and to ridicule the authorities.

Dolan's job is to inform the reader about the basic facts of the incident. This is not the same as explaining, where the writer will go into more depth to provide details of a particular idea. An example would be an exploration of the "elf and safety' culture mentioned in the article's heading, with the writer perhaps drawing upon his own opinions as well as factual evidence.

The article:

- is summarised in its headline
- is summarised again in its opening paragraph in slightly more detail
- uses the rest of its length to fill in the background
- answers the standard journalism questions: Who? What? Where? When? Why? (Richard Tremelling – Sacked – Swansea – 2009 – Allowed pupils to sledge)
- uses very short paragraphs, most of which consist of a single sentence
- often includes short, grammatically simple sentences ('The boys were unharmed.' 'He was dismissed in January last year.')
- quotes three people (Nick Seaton, Philip Davies, Lord Young) who are not in favour of the way current health and safety rules are dealt with in schools
- gives a lot of space (nine paragraphs) to Mr Tremelling's own account of what happened
- gives much less space (three paragraphs) to what Rosa Fernandes told the General Teaching Council for Wales in presenting the case against Mr Tremelling
- includes extra pieces of information such as Mr Tremelling's salary and the number of pupils in the school by building them into sentences as adjectival phrases
- quotes emotive words (chosen to get the reader's sympathy and agreement) such as 'disgraceful', 'ludicrous', 'heavy-handed', 'obsession', 'overreaction' and 'bureaucracy' to support the suggestion that Mr Tremelling has been treated unfairly.

Exercise 6.12

Write a *Daily Mail*-style news report relating to an incident, experimenting with some of the techniques used here by Andy Dolan. You should choose to focus on something which has happened in school or something you've seen reported on television or via the internet. Or you might – an entertaining challenge this – pick an incident from a work of fiction and give it the *Daily Mail* treatment.

There are writing guidelines for this exercise in the answers. Look for the section at the end of the answers called 'Writing guidelines'.

Speaking and listening

1 Is risk an essential part of life? Discuss your views in a group of four or five. Then join another group. Share your opinions.

2 Prepare a three- to four-minute presentation about an unusual, high-risk sport, using computer software if you wish and if it's available. Give your presentation to the rest of the class.

3 Invite into school a speaker from the Royal Society for the Prevention of Accidents (RoSPA). Ask him or her to talk about managing risk. Introduce your guest to the rest of the class and be prepared to ask thoughtful questions.

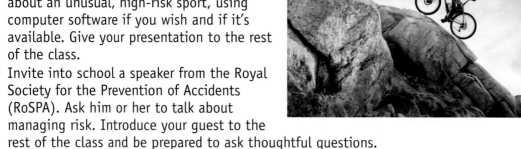

4 Work in a pair or a group of three. Re-read 'The Lotos-Eaters' as if you were risk assessors. Discuss all the dangers which faced the sailors. What could they have done to reduce risk?

Extra reading

These books all relate to the theme of risk, adventure and exploration in fiction or real life:

- *Bruised* by Siobhán Parkinson (2011)
- *The Storm Garden* by Philip Gross (2006)
- *A Walk in the Woods* by Bill Bryson (1998)
- *The Kite Rider* by Geraldine McCaughrean (2001)
- *Taking on the World* by Ellen MacArthur (2002)
- *Grasshopper* by Barbara Vine (2000)
- *Race to the Pole* by Ranulph Fiennes (2004)
- *Into the Crocodile Nest* by Benedict Allen (1987)
- *Faber Book of Exploration*, edited by Benedict Allen (2002)
- *The Report* by Jessica Francis Kane (2011)
- *The Birthday Boys* by Beryl Bainbridge (1996)
- *The Vault* by Ruth Rendell (2011)
- *Seven Years in Tibet* by Heinrich Harrer (1952)*
- *The Small Woman* by Alan Burgess (1957)*

*Recommended for very keen readers and for those taking scholarship

Progress further

- Barbara Vine mentions three architects: Lutyens, Mackintosh and Voysey. Find out about them. Use books or the internet. Look at some pictures of their work. Why did they become famous and why are they still remembered?

- Find a newspaper story (news or a feature) which uses a lot of quotations. Analyse it to see which quotes are examples of direct speech and which of indirect speech. Work out why you think the journalist has made the choices that he/she has.

- Alfred Lord Tennyson was Queen Victoria's Poet Laureate for most of her long reign. Find out about Tennyson's life and home on the Isle of Wight near the Queen's holiday home and share your findings with the rest of the class.

7 Family

Gran

Clay, the narrator of this story, lives with her parents, sister, brother and grandmother to whom she is very close. She is feeling uneasy and thinking about Gran who is away.

What had happened that evening wouldn't have happened if Gran had been there. I wished she'd ring but I knew she wouldn't. The last time she'd called she said that she and Beatrice were going to the beach for a few days. I pictured them sitting by their fire on the sand, next to the Pacific Ocean, under a sky full
5   of stars, drinking wine, happily smoking whatever they were smoking. I wanted to be there, not with Gran, to be Gran, to have jumped half a century, not looking forward to all the things I would be able to do but looking back on all the things I had done, without having done them.

That would be cheating. Gran said she'd earned the right to do what she liked
10   without caring what anyone else thought. And she *had* earned it. The joke about running off to a tepee in Wales, even if it was a caravan in Shropshire, wasn't really a joke. When she was at university she found she was pregnant, and her parents were very sympathetic until they found out that she and her boyfriend didn't intend to marry or even stay together. They thought she would have the
15   baby adopted and when she refused they told her not to come home until she changed her mind, and she never did. Never changed her mind and never went home again. Mum didn't know her grandparents and the man we'd always called Grandad wasn't, in fact, our grandfather. Mum was three when Gran married him. By then she had managed to get a teaching qualification and was working
20   and everything was fine.

But the joke about the bridge players wasn't all that funny either. Mum said he'd been a wonderful father to her but she often wondered if the reason he'd been happy to take her on was because he couldn't have any children of his own. He'd had mumps when he was thirteen and it had left him sterile. There was no IVF
25   treatment or sperm donation then. As well as being an accountant he was an amateur athlete and full of energy, and they'd travelled all over the place on holidays while Mum was growing up – and then he started playing bridge. Mum said it transformed him, it was almost as if he were addicted – well I suppose he was. Gran stayed with him, bored out of her skull, for five years until he died –
30   of monomania, Gran said, but it was a heart attack. I can remember him up to

the time I was about eight, being all the things Mum said he was, a wonderful grandfather the way he'd been a wonderful father, and then they went to the Isle of Wight and after that I can't remember him at all. He switched himself off.

35 After he died Gran discovered that it hadn't just been bridge. One thing led to another, poker, casinos, he'd been gambling heavily, that was the monomania, the addiction. He'd run up hideous debts and remortgaged the house without telling her. She was left with nothing. We didn't talk about these things, we just knew them, they were Gran's back story, and Mum's; the things that had made them what they were.

From *Turbulence* by Jan Mark (2005)

Exercise 7.1

Read the extract from *Turbulence* and answer the following questions:

1 What is Gran doing at the time of the story?

2 Why did Gran quarrel with her parents?

3 Why did Gran and her husband have no children of their own?

4 Where did Gran have to live after she broke away from her parents?

5 What was the 'monomania' that the narrator says her step-grandfather suffered from? How and where did it start?

6 Why and how does the narrator envy her grandmother? Use quotations from the passage to support your answer.

'We Are Seven'

A simple Child,
That lightly draws its breath,
And feels its life on every limb,
What should it know of death?

5 I met a little cottage Girl:
She was eight years old, she said;
Her hair was thick with many a curl
That clustered round her head.

She had a rustic, woodland air,
10 And she was wildly clad:
Her eyes were fair, and very fair;
Her beauty made me glad.

'Sisters and brothers, little Maid,
How many may you be?'
15 'How many? Seven in all,' she said,
And wondering looked at me.

'And where are they? I pray you tell.'
She answered, 'Seven are we;
And two of us at Conway dwell,
20 And two are gone to sea.

'Two of us in the church-yard lie,
My sister and my brother;
And, in the church-yard cottage, I
Dwell near them with my mother.'

25 'You say that two at Conway dwell,
And two are gone to sea,
Yet ye are seven! I pray you tell,
Sweet Maid, how this may be.'

Then did the little Maid reply,
30 'Seven boys and girls are we;
Two of us in the church-yard lie,
Beneath the church-yard tree.'

'You run about, my little Maid,
Your limbs they are alive;
35 If two are in the church-yard laid,
Then ye are only five.'

'Their graves are green, they may be seen,'
The little Maid replied,
'Twelve steps or more from my mother's door,
40 And they are side by side.

'My stockings there I often knit,
When it is light and fair,
I take my little porringer,
And eat my supper there.

45 'The first that died was sister Jane;
In bed she moaning lay,
Till God released her of her pain;
And then she went away.

'So in the church-yard she was laid;
50 And, when the grass was dry,

Together round her grave we played,
My brother John and I.

'And when the ground was white with snow,
And I could run and slide,
55 My brother John was forced to go,
And he lies by her side.'

'How many are you, then,' said I,
'If they two are in heaven?'
Quick was the little Maid's reply,
60 'O Master! We are seven.'

'But they are dead; those two are dead!
Their spirits are in heaven!'
'Twas throwing words away; for still
The little Maid would have her will,
65 And said, 'Nay we are seven!'

William Wordsworth (1798)

Exercise 7.2

Read the poem 'We Are Seven' and answer the following questions:

1 Account, in your own words, for the seven children in the little girl's family.

2 What does she say which interests the narrator so much?

3 Summarise the child's appearance in your own words.

4 What do you notice about Wordsworth's word choices in this poem?

5 What is the real 'message and mood' of this poem? Use direct quotation to support your views.

My mother

My mother's family came from Leamington Spa. I have a photograph of my grandfather fishing; surrounded by his three daughters and a formidable wife, he's wearing a sort of cricketing cap, a starched collar and a tweed jacket. He was, like my father's blindness, a taboo subject and no one ever said much about him
5 except that he was called Mr Smith and his profession was, as my father said with the sole purpose of irritating my mother, a 'bum-bailiff' or Warwickshire debt-collector. I have no idea why he shot himself, but my mother, at the end of her

life, told me that it happened while she had a job as a schoolmistress in South Africa. She learnt of it because her family sent her out a copy of the local paper
10 with the announcement of her father's death carefully marked as a news item which might interest her. From what she told me I understood that they sent no covering letter.

My mother had studied art in Birmingham, to which city she bicycled daily. Later she taught drawing in Manchester, at a Lycée in Versailles, and at a girls'
15 school in Natal, where she rode bareback across the veldt and swam naked under waterfalls. She was a 'New Woman' who read Bernard Shaw and Katherine Mansfield, whom she resembled a little in looks. My grandmother was a High Church Anglican whose bedside table supported a prayer-book and a crucifix, but my mother had no use at all for God, although she was to become revered as a
20 heroine and a saint in her middle age.

She earned these titles, of course, for putting up with my father; an almost impossible task.

From *Clinging to the Wreckage* by John Mortimer (1982)

Exercise 7.3

Read the extract from *Clinging to the Wreckage* and answer the following questions:

1 What is a 'taboo subject' (line 4)?

2 Why, do you infer, was 'putting up with my father … an almost impossible task' for the writer's mother?

3 What were the circumstances in which the writer's mother learnt of her father's death?

4 What were the writer's mother's religious beliefs?

5 Explain the meaning of the words (a) formidable (line 2) and (b) revered (line 19).

6 Summarise in your own words the impression you have of John Mortimer's mother.

Writing practice   Exercise 7.4

1 Write about your family or a family known to you.

2 Write a short story called 'Turbulence', treating the subject in any way you wish.

3 Write a story or a poem about a family coping either with death or disability.

4 Imagine you are Clay's gran. Write your granddaughter a letter from the Pacific coast of America.

5 Write the newspaper article which John Mortimer's mother received in South Africa. Add additional details about her father's life and family, if you wish.

6 Write your response to 'We Are Seven'. Comment on Wordsworth's choice of words, his rhyme scheme and the point of view he is exploring. Remember to first provide factual information about the poem before explaining its aspects in further detail.

Did you know?

These facts relate to the writers or topics featured in this chapter:

- The average age for becoming a great-grandparent is 75 (*Guardian*, 2007).

- There were 17.1 million families in Britain in 2006.

- John Mortimer was the father of actress and writer Emily Mortimer.

- Two is the most common number of children in British families but, because there are fewer very large families than there used to be, the average number is now 1.8.

Exercise 7.5

Research and note three separate facts to add to the list above. They should relate to families or to the writers and other topics touched on in this chapter. You should be able to summarise each of your facts in a single sentence.

Grammar and punctuation

Placement of only

Look at these sentences:

- **She only grew carrots.** (She didn't do anything else to carrots. She didn't buy them, or eat them or use them to make prints in art. All she did was to grow them.)
- **She grew only carrots** or **She grew carrots only.** (She didn't grow, for example, potatoes, runner beans or flowers. Carrots alone were what she grew.)
- **Only she grew carrots** or **She, only, grew carrots.** (Perhaps other people grew other things but she was the only grower of carrots.)

The position of the adverb 'only' changes the meaning and sometimes, as in the third example above, the punctuation changes it too.

Many speakers and writers are very careless with this, often using the first example when they mean the second.

Think carefully about what you mean and get into the habit of placing 'only' accurately.

Exercise 7.6

Write out these sentences, explaining in brackets what each means:

1 Only we read 'We Are Seven' that morning.

2 We only read 'We Are Seven' that morning.

3 We read only 'We Are Seven' that morning.

4 We read 'We Are Seven' only that morning.

5 *Turbulence* is the only novel by Jan Mark that I have read.

6 *Turbulence* is the novel by Jan Mark that only I have read.

7 *Turbulence* is the novel by Jan Mark that I have only read.

Split infinitive

In English we form the infinitive or 'title' of a verb with the word 'to'. The infinitive form does not have a tense or person or stated subject. So 'to walk', 'to play', 'to sing' and so on are infinitives.

We use them all the time by hooking them onto other verbs in sentences such as 'I need **to buy** some food' or 'Shall we get ready **to swim**?'

In other languages, such as French or Latin, infinitives are usually single words: *marcher* and *ambulare* ('to walk'), *jouer* and *ludere* ('to play'), *chanter* and *canere* ('to sing').

Because in English the infinitive is a two-word structure, other words – usually adverbs – sometimes get slipped into the middle. This is the famous **split infinitive** such as 'to boldly go' or 'to happily wait'.

Some people get very excited about split infinitives and regard them as the worst grammatical mistake you can make.

On the whole they are rather inelegant and it is much better to avoid them if possible. But sometimes trying to avoid the split infinitive gives you such a clumsy sentence that the split is better than the alternative. It's a matter of common sense.

Exercise 7.7

Rewrite each of these sentences without the split infinitive:

1 We must be sure to carefully prepare for the exam.

2 Are you ready to quickly visit Gran?

3 Mum told us that she used to only like reading books about horses.

4 I really will try to regularly practise the trumpet.

5 Let's get ready to really enjoy ourselves.

6 Americans seem to often use split infinitives.

Why do we need punctuation?

Look at these two sentences carefully:

● The policeman said, 'The accused is lying. I saw him break into the shop on Thursday night.'
● 'The policeman,' said the accused, 'is lying. I saw him break into the shop on Thursday night.'

The words are the same. But the meaning is completely changed by the punctuation.

Exercise 7.8

Make up six pairs of sentences of your own. In each pair the words should be exactly the same but punctuate them differently to change the meaning.

Spelling and vocabulary

mono- and -mania words

Monomania means an obsession ('mania') with a single thing ('mono') – in the case of the narrator's step-grandfather in the extract from *Turbulence* it was gambling.

Some -mania words are very well established, such as:

● **megalomania** (obsession with power)
● **kleptomania** (obsessive stealing)
● **dipsomania** (obsessive drinking or alcoholism).

Journalists and others often coin new -mania words, neologisms, to cater for the ever-increasing range of new obsessions, such as:

● **Euromania** (great enthusiasm for Europe or the European Union)

- **lotterymania** (obsession with lotteries)
- **Beatlemania** (obsession with the Beatles).

■ Waxwork figures of The Beatles in Madame Tussauds, Berlin

Some of these words stick and become a permanent part of the ever-changing language. Others disappear quite quickly.

Words which include the prefix mono- include:

- **monorail** (train track consisting of a single rail)
- **monocle** (single eye glass used instead of a pair of glasses)
- **monotone** (a sound using only one pitch).

Exercise 7.9

Copy out these words. Write a short definition for each of them.

1 monologue
2 bibliomania
3 monogamy
4 monochrome

5 trichotillomania
6 monolingual
7 monosyllable
8 pyromania

More silent letters

In some words (those which derive from Ancient Greek) the 'h' in 'ch' is silent – as in **chemist**, **character** or **orchid** (although there are plenty of other 'ch' words in English such as 'church' and 'chimpanzee' in which the 'h' is sounded). When you are writing these silent 'h' words do not forget to put the 'h' in, for instance in 'chaos' and 'orchestra'.

Similarly, some words from Ancient Greek use an 'rh' in which the 'h' is silent. These include **rhubarb**, **rheumatism** and **rhinoceros**. Make sure you spell them correctly.

Exercise 7.10

Illustrate the meaning of the following words by using each in a sentence. Learn (or revise) the spelling as you work:

1 rhizome

2 charismatic

3 rhapsody

4 rhombus

5 chorus

6 chiropodist

7 chemotherapy

8 chlorine

Functions of language

Humorous language

The British sense of humour is famous all over the world. It is quirky and often involves people or characters healthily laughing at themselves or seeing 'the funny side' of very serious issues. It often depends on understatement and can be quite subtle. This type of humour is rarely full of 'belly laugh' jokes or 'slapstick' comedy in which, for instance, people knock each other over or throw custard pies at each other. It is often related to words and language, spoken or written. It tends to be the kind of humour which makes you grin rather than roar with laughter.

British humour often pokes fun at the social class system (think of classic TV comedy like *Only Fools and Horses* or *To the Manor Born*). John Mortimer hints at it in his *Clinging to the Wreckage*. His father was a senior barrister and his father's father a high court judge while his mother's father was a debt-collector, named 'Mr Smith'. The writer's father cannot resist commenting on this class difference by referring to his father-in-law as a 'bum-bailiff' 'with the sole purpose of irritating my mother'.

John Mortimer's style is a good example of the British sense of humour. He:

- uses short sentences which sometimes seem disjointed ('My mother's family came from Leamington Spa.')
- sounds serious (although he isn't)
- uses very precise, formal language to highlight how inconsequential it all is ('to which city she bicycled daily', 'whose bedside table supported'); the precision of the language does not relate to the triviality of what he's describing, which turns it into a joke
- has fun with incongruous contrasts (Leamington Spa is very English and polite compared with naked swimming in South Africa)
- doesn't dwell on the terrible time his mother must have had looking after his father, but hints at it and makes it into an understated joke; laughing at, and making light of their hardships
- recalls how the only indication that his mother was given of her father's suicide was a newspaper cutting without a covering note – an example of black humour.

Exercise 7.11

Write a paragraph or two about a relative or someone you know, making it as understatedly funny as you can. Use some of the techniques which John Mortimer uses.

◯ Speaking and listening

1 Work in a group of four or five. Each one of you is a family member. Role-play an argument about homework.
2 Work with a partner. Devise a short play (sketch) based on 'We Are Seven'.
3 Tell a partner about a member of your family who is interesting, tiresome, entertaining, eccentric, charismatic, etc. (Everyone has at least one!) Then join another pair. Each of you should describe his or her partner's relative to the rest of the group.
4 Organise a discussion (or formal debate) on the question 'Is the traditional family disappearing and, if so, what are the effects of the change?'
5 Present an oral book review (perhaps on one of the titles recommended in this chapter or elsewhere in this book) to a small group or to the rest of the class.

Extra reading

These books all have family as a major theme:

- *The Truth about Celia Frost* by Paula Rawsthorne (2011)
- *Turbulence* by Jan Mark (2005)
- *Buddy* by Nigel Hinton (1982)
- *Looking for X* by Deborah Ellis (1999)
- *Falling Leaves Return to their Roots* by Adeline Yen Mah (1997)
- *Clinging to the Wreckage* by John Mortimer (1982)
- *No and Me* by Delphine de Vigan (2007)
- *Hungry Hill* by Daphne du Maurier (1943)
- *Germinal* by Emile Zola (1885)*
- *A Year Without Autumn* by Liz Kessler (2011)*
- *What Maisie Knew* by Henry James (1897)*
- *Anna Karenina* by Leo Tolstoy (1877)*

*Recommended for very keen readers and for those taking scholarship

Progress further

- Find out about the life and work of William Wordsworth. He believed that poetry should be about the everyday lives of ordinary people like the little girl in 'We Are Seven' – an unusual approach in the late eighteenth century when he started writing.

- John Mortimer (1923–2009) was a defence barrister. He gave up practising law to be a full-time writer of plays, TV and film scripts, and books. Read at least one of his books. He was a very witty writer.

- Compulsive gambling is a recognised addiction. Invite a representative of Gamblers Anonymous into school to tell you about the work of this organisation and the problems faced by its members.

- Research the changing role of grandparents in different cultures. Present your findings to the rest of the class.

⑧ Government

The Battle of the Windmill

A group of farm animals has evicted the farmer and other human beings. It now runs its own farm, but there are leadership problems and it is difficult to know whom to trust and who is telling the truth. And sometimes the farm is attacked by outsiders.

They had won, but they were weary and bleeding. Slowly they began to limp back towards the farm. The sight of their dead comrades stretched upon the grass moved some of them to tears. And for a little while they halted in sorrowful silence at the place where the windmill had once stood. Yes, it was
5 gone; almost the last trace of their labour was gone. Even the foundations were partially destroyed. And in rebuilding it they could not this time, as before, make use of the fallen stones. This time the stones had vanished too. The force of the explosion had flung them to distances of hundreds of yards. It was as though the windmill had never been.

10 As they approached the farm Squealer, who had unaccountably been absent during the fighting, came skipping towards them, whisking his tail and beaming with satisfaction. And the animals heard, from the direction of the farm buildings, the solemn boom of a gun.

'What is that gun firing for?' said Boxer.

15 'To celebrate our victory!' cried Squealer.

'What victory?' said Boxer. His knees were bleeding, he had lost a shoe and split his hoof, and a dozen pellets had lodged themselves in his hindleg.

'What victory, comrade? Have we not driven the enemy off our soil – the sacred soil of Animal Farm?'

20 'But they have destroyed the windmill. And we had worked on it for two years!'

'What matter? We will build another windmill. We will build six windmills if we feel like it. You do not appreciate, comrade, the mighty thing we have done. The enemy was in occupation of this very ground that we stand upon. And now – thanks to the leadership of Comrade Napoleon – we have won every inch of it
25 back again!'

'Then we have won back what we had before,' said Boxer.

'That is our victory,' said Squealer.

30 They limped into the yard. The pellets under the skin of Boxer's leg smarted painfully. He saw ahead of him the painful labour of rebuilding the windmill from the foundations, and already in imagination he braced himself for the task. But for the first time it occurred to him that he was eleven years old and that perhaps his great muscles were not quite what they had been.

35 But when the animals saw the green flag flying, and heard the gun firing again – seven times it was fired in all – and heard the speech that Napoleon made, congratulating them on their conduct, it did seem to them after all that they had won a great victory. The animals slain in battle were given a solemn funeral. Boxer and Clover pulled the wagon which served as a hearse, and Napoleon himself walked at the head of the procession. Two whole days were given over to celebrations. There were songs, speeches, and more firing of the gun, and a special
40 gift of an apple was bestowed on every animal, with two ounces of corn for each bird and three biscuits for each dog. It was announced that the battle would be known as the Battle of the Windmill, and that Napoleon had created a new decoration, the Order of the Green Banner, which he had conferred upon himself.

From *Animal Farm* by George Orwell (1945)

Exercise 8.1

Read the extract from *Animal Farm* and answer the following questions:

1 What had the animals been doing immediately before this passage opens and what is the result?

2 What is implied by 'Squealer, who had unaccountably been absent during the fighting'?

3 Who is Napoleon and what impression do you get of him from this passage?

4 What do you learn from this passage about Boxer's character? Support your answer with direct quotations.

5 Why does Squealer address the other animals as 'comrade'?

6 Think about why this passage has been included in this chapter about government. Is this extract really about animals? Give reasons for your answer.

Uneasy lies the head that wears a crown

In Shakespeare's play *Henry IV Part 2* it is the middle of the night, but the old king cannot sleep. He is worried about his kingdom and his son. He is also ill.

King Henry IV:

How many thousand of my poorest subjects
Are at this hour asleep! O sleep, O gentle sleep,
Nature's soft nurse, how have I frighted thee,
That thou no more wilt weigh my eyelids down
5 And steep my senses in forgetfulness?
Why rather, sleep, liest thou in smoky cribs,
Upon uneasy pallets stretching thee
And hushed with buzzing night-flies to thy slumber,
Than in the perfumed chambers of the great,
10 Under the canopies of costly state,
And lulled with sound of sweetest melody?
O thou dull god, why liest thou with the vile
In loathsome beds, and leavest the kingly couch
A watch-case or a common 'larum-bell?
15 Wilt thou upon the high and giddy mast
Seal up the ship-boy's eyes, and rock his brains
In cradle of the rude imperious surge,
And in the visitation of the winds,
Who take the ruffian billows by the top,
20 Curling their monstrous heads, and hanging
them With deafing clamour in the slippery
clouds, That with the hurly death itself
awakes? Canst thou, O partial sleep, give thy
repose To the wet sea-boy in an hour so rude,
25 And in the calmest and most stillest night,
With all the appliances and means to boot,
Deny it to a king? Then happy low, lie down!
Uneasy lies the head that wears a crown.

From *Henry IV Part 2* by William Shakespeare (1600)

Exercise 8.2

Read the extract from *Henry IV Part 2* and answer the following questions:

1 Why does King Henry envy his subjects?

2 To whom or what is most of this speech addressed?

3 List synonyms for bed(s) which Shakespeare gives Henry to use in this
   passage. Evaluate what they add to the piece.

4 Why does he mention the ship-boy?

5 Choose two examples of alliteration, assonance or consonance (see page 136)
   in this speech and say why they are effective.

6 Explain in your own words what Henry means by 'Uneasy lies the head that
   wears a crown'.

Gaddafi: tyrant or benign ruler?

Colonel Gaddafi ruled Libya from 1969 until 2011 when, in August, he was
overthrown by rebels supported by NATO forces. Two months later he was
caught and shot. Read these two very different accounts of him, both taken from
obituaries. Then answer the questions which follow.

Passage A

Colonel Omar Mohammad Gaddafi was the Head of the Libyan State, Chairman
of the Revolutionary Command Council, co-founder and longtime chairman of
the African Union, and author of the Third International Theory which served as
the basis of the Islamic Socialist Republic of Libya, and an inspiration to anti-
5 Western causes across Arabia.

Gaddafi was a unique and defiant ruler who died as a warrior-king, upholding
the highest honor a man can possibly achieve: martyrdom against his blood-
enemy. Against an insurmountable foe and against all possible odds, Omar
fought to the death against the invading CIA mercenaries and foreign usurpers.
10 For much of his life Omar had cursed Western arrogance. He continued to stand
in defiance of their aggression until the very last moments of his life.

Gaddafi did not spend much money on his military and never accumulated
bio-chemical or nuclear weapons, which ultimately may have led to his demise.
Instead, he had invested in welfare programs and free colleges for students with
15 high grades.

His body was hidden in the southern deserts by the US military's hired goons.
Perhaps it is a fitting respite for a man who was born and raised among the
anonymous pathways of the Sahara. May you rest in peace, Colonel. I am one
American who will not forget your name.

Omar Mohammad Gaddafi 1942–2011 (martyred)

Abridged from an obituary by Reed Perry on reedperry.com (2011)

Passage B

Colonel Muammar Gaddafi, the former Libyan dictator who has been killed aged
69, liked to promote himself as an instigator of global revolution; for the four
decades of his rule, however, this was carried out through the subjugation of his
people at home, and the sponsorship of terrorism abroad.

5   His grip on power always looked solid. But in February 2011 the uprisings in
North Africa, which had already seen the fall of the governments of Libya's
neighbours, Egypt and Tunisia, suddenly put his regime in jeopardy.

It was a suitably chaotic end for a man who could never be easily pigeonholed.
Erratic, vain and utterly unpredictable, he always seemed to be enjoying a
10 private joke which no one else could see. His image, plastered on walls all over
Libya, seemed a parody of Sixties radical chic – the craggy features, longish hair,
the eyes half-hidden behind retro blue-tone shades.

Gaddafi would arrive at summits of Arab leaders in a white limousine
surrounded by a bodyguard of nubile Kalashnikov-toting brunettes. At one
15 non-aligned summit in Belgrade, he turned up with two horses and six camels;
the Yugoslavs allowed him to graze the camels in front of his hotel – where he
pitched his tent and drank fresh camel milk – but refused to allow him to arrive
at the conference on one of his white chargers. Several of the camels ended up
in Belgrade zoo.

20 At an African Union summit in Durban in 2002, his entourage consisted of a
personal jet, two Antonov transport aircraft, a container ship loaded with buses,
goat carcases and prayer mats, a mobile hospital, jamming equipment that
disrupted local networks, $6 million in petty cash, and 400 security guards with
associated rocket launchers, armoured cars and other hardware, who nearly
25 provoked a shoot-out with South Africa's security forces.

Yet the self-styled 'Universal Theorist' and 'Guide of the First of September
Great Revolution of the Arab Libyan Popular and Socialist Jamahiriya' was no
joke. In the 1970s and 1980s, while other tyrants were content to repress their
own people, Gaddafi seemed hell-bent on bringing murder and mayhem to the
30 whole world.

After PanAm Flight 103 was blown up over Lockerbie in 1988, leaving 270
dead – the biggest mass murder in British history – a court found two Libyans
guilty of planting the bomb on board. In 1984, WPC Yvonne Fletcher was shot
dead in London with a machine gun fired from inside the Libyan embassy. Then
35 there was the bombing of a Berlin discotheque, explosions at Rome and Vienna
airports and the bombing of a French airliner over Chad.

In addition, Gaddafi sent arms
shipments to the IRA, Abu Nidal,
and numerous other terrorist
40   organisations and set out to export
revolution to his neighbours,
perpetuating regional conflicts
in Sierra Leone, Zimbabwe, Chad
and Liberia. Domestic opponents
45   – the 'running dogs' who opposed
his dictatorship – were ruthlessly
liquidated. In 1984 bomb attacks on
seven Libyan exiles living in Britain

■ Muammar Gaddafi during a state visit to
Ukraine, 2008

left 24 people injured; one Libyan journalist opposed to Gaddafi's regime was
50   assassinated as he walked past London's Regent's Park mosque.

Colonel Muammar Gaddafi, born 1942, died 20 October 2011

Abridged from an obituary published in the *Daily Telegraph* (2011)

Exercise 8.3

1 What evidence is there in Passage A that the writer is American, apart from
the statement in his final sentence?

2 How, if you didn't know that the *Daily Telegraph* is a British newspaper, could
you deduce that Passage B is almost certainly the work of a British writer?

3 How old was Gaddafi when his rule started?

4 Give three examples from each passage (six in all) of words which suggest a
strong opinion.

5 Summarise in your own words, in two sentences for each, the view of Gaddafi
suggested by (a) Passage A and (b) Passage B.

6 Why does Passage B describe Gaddafi's travel arrangements in such detail?

7 What, according to Passage A, were Gaddafi's great strengths?

8 What does Passage B regard as Gaddafi's worst actions and policies?

9 Which of these two passages do you find more trustworthy and why? Quote
from the passages to support your answer.

Writing practice   Exercise 8.4

1 Using the facts given by the writers of Passage A and Passage B, write a
neutral summary of Colonel Gaddafi's life.

2 Now write out arguments both in favour of and against Colonel Gaddafi, and
conclude which arguments are stronger, and why.

3   You are a head of state (in any country or an imaginary one) who cannot sleep. Write your thoughts in prose or poetry.

4   Boxer of *Animal Farm* is a carthorse. Write an interview with him for a magazine after the Battle of the Windmill.

5   Write a story about a group of animals doing something original or unexpected.

6   Write about government in any way you wish.

7   You are one of Henry IV's servants. Write a letter home to your family about your employer's health and state of mind. Use some of the detail from the passage and as much imagination as you wish.

Did you know?

These facts relate to the writers or topics featured in this chapter:

- George Orwell's real name was Eric Blair.

- Queen Victoria, who became Queen aged 18 in 1837 and died in 1901, held the record for the longest reigning British monarch until 9 September 2015 when she was overtaken by Queen Elizabeth II.

- Shakespeare was fascinated by tyrants. Other plays which explore the nature of tyranny include *Macbeth*, *Julius Caesar* and *Measure for Measure*.

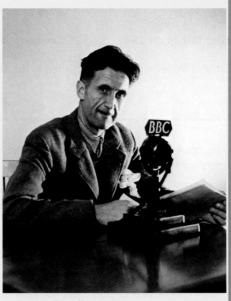
■ George Orwell in 1943

Exercise 8.5

Research and note three separate facts to add to the list above. They should relate to government or to the writers and other topics touched on in this chapter. You should be able to summarise each of your facts in a single sentence.

◯ Grammar and punctuation

Common errors

1 'Fewer' can be used only for something which you can count, e.g. days, meals, items, books. 'Less' is used to qualify something which cannot be counted or quantified, e.g. water, colour, excitement. So:
   - fewer cars but less traffic
   - fewer cartons but less milk.

   There are some exceptions where 'fewer' sounds awkward, for example you wouldn't say: 'I have fewer than ten pounds left.' Also watch out for cases where the phrase 'more or less' is used.

2 Avoid tautology – using unnecessary words which repeat something you've already said.

   For example, you need never write or say 'return back' because 'to return' means 'to go back'. The word 'back' here would be tautologous. Similarly, you don't need to 'ascend up' a hill or 'shout loudly' either.

3 The verb 'to lay' is transitive. So it requires an object. You can, for instance, lay a table, a trail, bricks or carpets. So:
   - Our hens are **laying** (or have **laid**, were **laying**, etc.) nice, big brown eggs.

   But the verb 'to lie' has two meanings and is never transitive. It means (a) to tell an untruth and (b) to be in a horizontal position. So:
   - He **lies** all the time about his family.
   - In summer I often **lie** on a rug in the garden to read.

   But take care. The past tense of the second meaning of the verb 'to lie' confuses some people so that they muddle it with the verb 'to lay'. Learn:
   - A servant helped Henry **lie** on the bed.
   - Henry IV **lay** dying.
   - He had **lain** sleepless for several hours.

   'Layed' does not exist. And if you don't hurry to get up on a non-school day you are, of course, having a **lie-in**, not a 'lay-in' which doesn't exist either.

Exercise 8.6

Write out these sentences putting 'fewer' or 'less' into the spaces:

1 George Orwell wrote _____ books than Charles Dickens.

2 Do we need more or _____ suitcases for this year's holiday?

3 We have _____ luggage than usual.

4 In the end Gaddafi had _____ supporters than he needed in Libya.

5 This queue is for shoppers with _____ than eight items to pay for.

6 There is _____ traffic on the M25 after about eight o'clock.

7 I am trying to eat _____ .

8 That means I munch _____ chocolate bars.

Exercise 8.7

Use the verbs 'to lay' or 'to lie' to complete these sentences. You will need various parts of the verbs and different tenses.

1 'Please don't _____ to me,' said the headmaster.

2 Let's _____ on the beach and rest for a while.

3 The old man had _____ on the floor for an hour before he was found.

4 Our new carpet was very well _____ .

5 'Let us _____ these _____ to rest,' said the policeman, trying to get at the truth.

6 Black Colombian hens _____ the best eggs.

7 'I don't enjoy a _____ in,' _____ Thomas.

8 While the twins _____ on the sofa resting, Mum _____ out their party clothes.

Exercise 8.8

Rewrite these sentences without tautology:

1 I want to re-read *Henry IV Part 1* again.

2 Muammar Gaddafi was never chosen as the elected ruler of Libya.

3 After the Battle of the Windmill, the animals were also very tired as well.

4 In a little while I shall change my library books later.

5 All formal invitations should be replied back to.

6 Before exams it's a good idea to revise over your work.

Punctuation revision

Exercise 8.9

Punctuate these passages as a way of revising your understanding of the rules of punctuation:

1 years passed the seasons came and went the short animal lives fled by a time came when there was no one who remembered the old days before the

rebellion except clover benjamin moses the raven and a number of pigs (From *Animal Farm* by George Orwell)

2 the letter from guy was still on the desk where i had left it wondering why i had bothered to keep it once i had read it i tore it up and dropped the pieces in our waste bin silver watching me said are you going to am i going to what marry him this guy guy i could hardly believe it i stared at him of course im not going to marry him im too young to get married (From *Grasshopper* by Barbara Vine)

3 oz is a big bloke and i am not small but it took our combined weight to shift whatever was behind the door far enough for oz to squeeze through i stayed outside and put my hand round it sandor was collapsed on the floor between the wash hand basin at one end and the lavatory at the other half sitting against the door feet against the opposite wall i couldn't see his face he didn't seem to be breathing is he dead i could only whisper it (From *Turbulence* by Jan Mark)

◯ Spelling and vocabulary

-some words

Shakespeare gives Henry IV the word **loathsome** – an adjective which describes something to be loathed.

Adjectives which have the suffix -some, from Old English, are interesting because their stems can be nouns (**burdensome**) or verbs (**loathsome**).

There are two groups:

- Adjectives which describe the state suggested by the stem – for example, an **adventuresome** person likes adventure.
- Adjectives which mean something which induce the state suggested by the stem – for example, a **flavoursome** food has flavours for others to enjoy and a **fearsome** person frightens others.

There are also -some words, still in use, which stem from words which have changed their meaning. So **cumbersome** means 'clumsy' or 'awkward' because a 'cumber' is an old word for a burden or obstruction. Similarly **handsome** used to mean 'easy to handle'.

Journalists and others, fond of neologisms, sometimes coin new -some words too. **Toothsome** is a fairly recent word meaning 'tasty', and **cringesome** suggests someone or something who/which makes you cringe.

Exercise 8.10

Use the words below to complete the sentences:

wholesome	awesome	bothersome
irksome	tiresome	fulsome

1 Although the word '_____' is often misused it really does describe accurately most people's reaction to the Pyramids.

2 Midges can be very _____ in Scotland although some people are unaffected.

3 Traffic noise is _____ when it continues all night.

4 _____ food includes fruit, vegetables and home-cooked dishes.

5 Mr Jones's comments about my painting were so _____ and complimentary that I didn't really believe him.

6 Boxer and the other animals on Manor Farm found the rebuilding work _____.

Exercise 8.11

Explain the meaning of:

1 quarrelsome

2 winsome

3 venturesome

4 meddlesome

5 noisesome

6 wearisome

More silent letters

Some words in English from Ancient Greek such as **psalm, psychologist** and **pterodactyl** have a silent 'p'. In Greek the combination 'ps' is one letter, psi (ψ). Similarly, the combination 'ch' (found in words such as **chorus, Christmas, technical**, etc.) is one letter, **chi** (χ).

Functions of language

Satire

Animal Farm is a satirical novel. George Orwell, tongue in cheek, called it a 'fairy story'. He is using satire to make a very serious point by showing animals being taken advantage of by cleverer and more powerful animals. Their leaders – the pigs – fool them. Orwell is using his animals to show truths, as he sees them, about politics and government.

Here is another example of satirical writing:

'If you want to get nicked, get a hat'

I don't need to tell you what the greatest scourge of our times is. As you all know it is old ladies. The older they are the more evil and criminal they tend to be. And the really shocking ones are easily spotted, for they are inevitably to be found wearing that ultimate symbol of violence and depravity, the hat. So full marks to
5 the Hereward pub in Ely for spotting an obvious trouble-maker, 82-year-old Betty Wilbraham, when she pushed her luck, took a diabolical liberty and attempted to enter their premises wearing a titfer.

As the pub pointed out, public safety could properly be preserved only if Mrs Wilbraham removed the hat. She could then be easily identified on security
10 cameras when she started to break bottles and smash the place up – as old ladies like her inevitably tend to do. Mrs Wilbraham, rather perplexed, says that she always wears a hat and that her late mother 'wouldn't have set foot outside the house without wearing one'. So what they say about criminal dynasties is clearly true, then.

From an article written by Simon Heffer and published in the *Daily Telegraph* (2006)

Simon Heffer:

- uses a 'deadpan' style pretending to believe what he says ('as you all know'), borrowing the language usually associated with criticism of youthful bad behaviour ('shocking', 'depravity', 'smash the place up', 'criminal dynasties')
- chooses exaggerated language ('a diabolical liberty')
- actually means the opposite of what he says ('So full marks')
- is fiercely critical of the Hereward pub
- sympathises with Mrs Wilbraham
- uses humour and irony to make his point ('as old ladies like her inevitably tend to do').

Exercise 8.12

Write a short piece using satire and irony to criticise, or make fun of, something or someone. Use some of the techniques Simon Heffer uses.

◯ Speaking and listening

1 Work in a group of three. One of you is Reed Perry (writer of Passage A on page 99), another is the *Daily Telegraph* obituary writer (pages 100–101) and the third is a radio presenter. Work out your conversation concerning Gaddafi's life and legacy.

2 Learn by heart the speech (soliloquy) from *Henry IV Part 2*. Then work out how to speak it to make it as compelling as possible.

3 Organise a discussion or debate about the present government. What is right or wrong with it? How could it be better? Don't talk about the personalities and private lives of politicians. Try to concentrate on policies. Use newspapers and the internet as sources of information.

4 Hold a balloon debate. Five people pretend to be famous or important people from the past or the present – such as William Shakespeare, Saint Francis, Nelson Mandela, Florence Nightingale and Sylvia Pankhurst. The imaginary balloon that they are all in is losing gas and dropping. The only way to save the lives of four people is to throw the fifth one out – otherwise everyone in the balloon will die. Each 'balloonist' makes a speech explaining why he/she is too important to the world to die. Then the rest of the class votes to decide who leaves the balloon and which four stay in.

5 Tell the rest of the class about a book you have read recently, explaining why you enjoyed it and why you would recommend it.

Extra reading

These books feature various forms of government:

- *Animal Farm* by George Orwell (1945)
- *Across the Nightingale Floor* by Lian Hearn (2002)
- *The Chocolate War* by Robert Cormier (1974)
- *The Other Boleyn Girl* by Philippa Gregory (2001)
- *The Dogs of War* by Frederick Forsyth (1974)
- *A Matter of Loyalty* by Sandra Howard (2009)
- *A Week in December* by Sebastian Faulks (2009)
- *Wild Swans* by Jung Chang (1994)*

*Recommended for very keen readers and for those taking scholarship

Progress further

- In his 1946 essay 'Politics and the English Language' George Orwell suggested these six rules for clear, concise English:

  1 Never use a metaphor, simile or other figure of speech which you are used to seeing in print.

  2 Never use a long word where a short one will do.

  3 If it is possible to cut out a word, always cut it out.

  4 Never use the passive where you can use the active.

  5 Never use a foreign phrase, a scientific word or a jargon word if you can think of an everyday English equivalent.

  6 Break any of these rules sooner than say anything outright barbarous.

  Look again at the extract from *Animal Farm* and consider how far Orwell followed his own rules. Now look at any article from a recent newspaper. To what extent is the journalist following Orwell's rules? Would it have been a better piece of writing if he or she had followed them more closely? Can you follow these rules in your own work?

- *Henry IV Part 2* is part of a sequence of 'history' plays by Shakespeare: *Richard II, Henry IV Part 1, Henry IV Part 2, Henry V*. Read some of them, see a performance or watch filmed versions. The BBC's *The Hollow Crown* series is the latest TV adaptations of these. Leon Garfield's *Shakespeare Stories* (1985) retell *Richard II* and *Henry IV Part 1*.

- Find out what you can about Libya, using reference books and the internet. Make a poster for the classroom wall to share some of what you have found out with others.

9 War

The front line

Stephen Wraysford is a junior officer in the First World War. He has been injured in the Battle of the Somme.

They emerged to find chaos. Further shelling had caused casualties in the trench and had destroyed the parapet over a length of fifty yards. They took what cover they could find. Byrne dragged Stephen's body to a relatively unscathed section while Hunt went in search of help. He was told that the regimental aid post,
5 supposedly impregnable in its dugout, had been wiped out by a direct hit.

Stephen lay on his side, with the wood of the duckboards against the skin of his face, his legs bent double by Byrne to keep him out of the way of men moving up and down. His face was covered with dirt, the pores plugged with fragments blown into them by the explosion of a German grenade. He had a piece of
10 shrapnel in his shoulder and had been hit by a rifle bullet in the neck; he was concussed by the blast and unconscious. Byrne pulled out his field dressing kit and emptied iodine into the hole in Stephen's neck; he found the tapes that pulled open the linen bag and freed the gauze dressing on its long bandage.

Rations came at ten o'clock. Byrne tried to force some rum between Stephen's
15 lips, but they would not open. In the bombardment priority was given to repairing defences and to moving the wounded who could walk. Stephen lay for a day in a niche dug for him by Byrne until a stretcher-bearer finally got him to a forward dressing station.

Stephen felt a profound weariness. He wanted to sleep in long draughts of days,
20 twenty at a time, in perfect silence. As the consciousness returned he seemed to manage only a shallow sleep. He dipped in and out of it and sometimes when he awoke he found his body had been moved. He was unaware of the pattering of rain on his face. Each time he awoke the pain seemed to have intensified.

He had the impression that time had gone into reverse and he was travelling
25 back closer to the moment of impact. Eventually time would stop at the moment the metal pierced his flesh and the pain would stay constant at that level. He yearned for sleep; with what willpower he could muster he forced away the waking world and urged himself into the darkness.

As infection set in, he began to sweat; the fever reached its height within
30   minutes, making his body shake and his teeth rattle. His muscles were convulsed
and his pulse began to beat with a fierce, accelerated rhythm. The sweat soaked
through his underclothes and mud-caked uniform.

By the time they had transported him to the dressing station the fever had started
to recede. The pain in his arm and neck had vanished. Instead he could hear a
35   roaring sound of blood in his ears. Sometimes it would modulate to a hum and
at others rise to a shriek according to how hard his heart was pumping. With the
noise came a delirium. He lost touch with his physical being and believed himself
to be in a house on a French boulevard in which he searched and called the name
of Isabelle. With no warning he was in an English cottage, a large institution, then
40   back in the unremembered place of his birth. He raved and shouted.

He could smell the harsh carbolic soap of the orphanage, then the schoolroom
with its dust and chalk. He was going to die without ever having been loved, not
once, not by anyone who had known him. He would die alone and unmourned.
He could not forgive them – his mother or Isabelle or the man who had
45   promised to be a father. He screamed.

'He's shouting for his mother,' said the orderly as they brought him into the tent.

'They always do,' said the medical officer, peeling back the field dressing Byrne
had applied almost thirty hours before.

They put him out of the tent to await transport to the casualty clearing station
50   or death, whichever should come first.

Then, under the indifferent sky his spirit left the body with its ripped flesh,
infections, its weak and damaged nature. While the rain fell on his arms and legs,
the part of him that still lived was unreachable. It was not his mind, but some
other essence that was longing now for peace on a quiet, shadowed road where
55   no guns sounded. The deep paths of darkness opened up for it, as they opened
up for other men along the lines of dug earth, barely fifty yards apart.

Then, as the fever in his abandoned body reached its height and he moved
towards the welcome of oblivion, he heard a voice, not human, but clear and
urgent. It was the sound of his life leaving him. Its tone was mocking. It offered
60   him, instead of the peace he longed for, the possibility of return. At this late
stage he could go back to his body and to the brutal perversion of life that
was lived in the turned soil and torn flesh of the war; he could, if he made
the effort of courage and will, come back to the awkward, compromised and
unconquerable existence that made up human life on earth. The voice was
65   calling him; it appealed to his sense of shame and of curiosity unfulfilled: but if
he did not heed it he would surely die.

From *Birdsong* by Sebastian Faulks (1993)

Exercise 9.1

Read the extract from *Birdsong* and answer the following questions:

1 Give other words or phrases for (a) unscathed (line 3), (b) impregnable (line 5), (c) modulate (line 35).

2 Describe Stephen's injuries.

3 How long was it before the men could get Stephen away from the fighting and what were the reasons?

4 Summarise Stephen's thoughts and ideas as he waits for treatment, in your own words.

5 Do you think Stephen will die? Give detailed reasons for your answer supported by quotations from the passage.

'Dulce et Decorum est'

Bent double, like old beggars under sacks,
Knock-kneed, coughing like hags, we cursed through sludge,
Till on the haunting flares we turned our backs
And towards our distant rest began to trudge.
5   Men marched asleep. Many had lost their boots
But limped on, blood-shod. All went lame; all blind
Drunk with fatigue; deaf even to the hoots
Of tired, outstripped Five-Nines[1] that dropped behind.

Gas! GAS! Quick, boys – An ecstasy of fumbling,
10   Fitting the clumsy helmets just in time;
But someone still was yelling out and stumbling
And flound'ring like a man in fire or lime...
Dim, through the misty panes and thick green light,
As under a green sea, I saw him drowning.

15   In all my dreams, before my helpless sight,
He plunges at me, guttering, choking, drowning.

If in some smothering dreams you too could pace
Behind the wagon we flung him in,
His hanging face, like a devil's sick of sin;
20   If you could hear, at every jolt, the blood
Come gargling from froth-corrupted lungs,
Obscene as cancer, bitter as the cud
Of vile, incurable sores on innocent tongues, –
My friend, you would not tell with such high zest

■ Soldiers in the First World War during a gas attack

25   To children ardent for some desperate glory,
       The old Lie: Dulce et decorum est
       Pro patria mori.[2]

Wilfred Owen (written in 1918 and
first published in 1920)

> [1] A very destructive German high-explosive shell
> [2] A Latin phrase which means 'It is sweet and right to die for your country'

Exercise 9.2

1 Describe in your own words what has happened to the man who is 'drowning'.

2 Why is it difficult for the men to walk? Illustrate your answer with quotations from the passage.

3 Why does Owen call the Latin tag 'The old Lie'?

4 Choose two of Owen's comparisons (metaphors, similes or other imagery) from the poem, comment on them and say why you think they are effective.

5 What do the rhyme and rhythm add to the poem as a whole?

100 Years Ago: Britain Enters the First World War

Professor Stephen Badsey, Professor of Conflict Studies at Wolverhampton University, reflects on Britain's entry to 'The Great War' in 1914.

     Looking back on the start of the First World War, we are conscious of a world and a Britain very different from our own. The countdown of events that led to Britain declaring war rings like a death-march in the heads of everyone who knows them. The war was precipitated by the assassination of Archduke Franz Ferdinand, heir to
5 the imperial throne, on Sunday 28 June in Sarajevo in Bosnia, recently officially annexed to Austria–Hungary, carried out by Serb nationalist terrorists backed by some members of the Serbian government. It was the third war in the Balkans in three years, in a time of tension and instability. This time, the declarations of war went further, involving the complex alliances between the great powers of
10 Europe. A month later, on Tuesday 28th July the Austro-Hungarian Empire declared war on Serbia, and next day bombarded the Serbian capital of Belgrade. Serbia's protector the Russian Empire mobilised its own forces, leading to the German Empire going to war in support of its ally Austria–Hungary, and invading Belgium as part of its war plan to defeat France as Russia's ally. Unable to tolerate

15 this, exactly a week after the Austro-Hungarian declaration, at 11.00 pm (London time) on Tuesday 4 August, the United Kingdom declared war against Germany. At the time it was called the European War or the Great War, involving all the major powers of Europe with their empires.

20 To modern eyes, the Britain that entered the First World War seems riven with paradoxes. It was a country of immense disparities, in which class distinctions were visible in the clothes that people wore, in which about one percent of the population owned seventy percent of its wealth, in which fewer than two men in three had the vote, and no women had the vote at all. Britain was the centre of the world's only global empire, many of whose subjects had no say at all in their
25 own governance. But Britain called itself a democracy, and so did its enemies – as an insult. It was a country of small communities and great regional variations, divided not only by accent and class but by politics, including increasing strikes by organised labour, violent protests by the women's suffrage movement, and the very real threat of a civil war in Ireland that distracted the British government
30 from events in Europe at a critical time. But in the crisis of the outbreak of the war, Britain also proved to be the strongest and most socially cohesive of all the major powers, able to raise an army of half a million men by the end of the year through volunteerism, with the capacity over four years both to outlast and outfight its enemies. Britain emerged from the First World War as one of the
35 victors, with its empire at its greatest ever extent, and its enemies defeated.

Our modern view of Britain in the First World War is concerned first of all with the dead; and for most British people they were always the most important part of the war at the time. Although no-one can say exactly how many Britons died as a direct result of the war, the number was around
40 three-quarters of a million, plus perhaps a further half-million from the wider British Empire, all unique human beings. But both in absolute numbers and as a proportion of the population, this was a smaller loss than either France or Germany, or any other major power. British deaths were far from being a 'lost generation'; they represented
45 just over one-twentieth of their age-group, comparable to levels of emigration from Britain over the previous decades. Proportionally, the
50 heaviest losses were suffered by the young men of the most privileged classes, who paid in blood for their privileges. Very few people greeted the
55 outbreak of the war with enthusiasm, but from start

to finish, for the great majority, it remained one of the most popular wars that Britain had ever fought. The actions and opinions of British dissenters from the war effort are important precisely because they were so rare and unusual.

60 The immense variations in individual experiences make it extremely difficult to make any generalisation about British opinions at the time, but it appears certain that the great majority of people believed that fighting and winning the First World War was worth it. If that seems strange or hard for us to understand, that is partly due to the war itself, and partly due to the hundred years' distance
65 from which we are looking at it.

From an article written by Professor Stephen Badsey, University of Wolverhampton (2014)

Exercise 9.3

1 Summarise in your own words the main topic under discussion in Professor Badsey's web article.

2 Which two points of view does he explore relating to this topic?

3 Explain the meaning of the words (a) annexed (line 6), (b) suffrage (line 28), (c) cohesive (line 31) and (d) dissenters (line 58).

4 Identify the phrases at the start of paragraphs 1, 2 and 3 that show which perspective the professor is taking.

5 In paragraph 2, where does he use contrasting language to emphasise each side of the discussion?

6 At what point in paragraph 3 does the focus shift from British deaths in the First World War to the comparative popularity of the war?

7 How effective do you find the conclusion? Use quotation from the final paragraph to support your answer.

Writing practice Exercise 9.4

1 Describe an occasion when you have been hurt or injured.

2 Imagine you are a young man fighting in France in 1915. Write a letter home to your sister.

3 Imagine you are Byrne in *Birdsong*. Write your diary for the day that Stephen Wraysford was injured.

4 Write an essay about 'Dulce et Decorum est'. Use some of the work you did in Exercise 9.2 to help you.

5 Write a story called 'Birdsong'.

6 Write about war in any way you wish.

(**Exercise 9.5**)

Research and note three separate facts to add to the list above. They should relate to war or to the writers and other topics touched on in this chapter. You should be able to summarise each of your facts in a single sentence.

○ Grammar and punctuation

Past participles

Past participles are formed from verbs to create the perfect (as opposed to the simple past) tense and can also be used like adjectives. If one breaks a chair, for example, the chair can be described as 'broken' ('broken' is the past participle of the verb 'to break'). They often need an auxiliary (or 'helping') verb, usually the verb 'to have'. For example:

● She has **arrived.**
● We have **wondered.**
● They had **asked.**

Most past participles in English are formed by adding 'd' or 'ed' to the root verb (e.g. 'marched', 'enquired'), sometimes after removing or changing a letter such as a 'y' (e.g. 'hurried', 'worried') or doubling a letter (e.g. 'pegged', 'tinned').

But many of our commonest verbs have irregular past participles. For example:

- He has **sung**.
- My father has **spoken**.
- You have **eaten**?

Note that in English the past tense of the verb uses a form which is often, but not always, identical to the past participle of the verb.

Thus:

verb	past tense	past participle
to walk	I walked	walked
to teach	I taught	taught

But note:

to swim	I ate	
to eat	swum	
I swam	eaten	

> In the seventeenth century the past participle of the verb 'to get' was 'gotten' (compare it with 'forget' and 'forgotten'). This has changed over time. In Britain we now use 'got' – e.g. 'Emma had got a dog.' Early migrants to America from England in the 1600s took the language with them and it has developed differently. For example, many Americans still say 'gotten' not 'got'.

Exercise 9.6

1 List 20 regular past participles that can follow 'I have…'

2 List 20 irregular past participles that can follow 'He has…'

3 Add an object if some of your verbs are transitive. For example: He has eaten my apple.

Revision

Below is some witty advice once given by a newspaper editor to his journalists because he wanted them to write clearly and well. If you have worked through all the exercises in this book you should have no difficulty working out what the editor means. His first ten rules for good writing are listed here. The other ten are included in Chapter 10.

1 Verbs has to agree with their subjects.
2 Prepositions are not words to end sentences with.
3 And don't start a sentence with a conjunction.
4 It is wrong to ever split an infinitive.
5 Avoid clichés like the plague.
6 Also, always avoid annoying alliteration.
7 Be more or less specific.
8 Parenthetical remarks (however relevant) are (usually) unnecessary.
9 No sentence fragments.
10 One should never generalise.

Exercise 9.7

Take the above rules one by one and explain the point which the editor is making.

◯ Spelling and vocabulary

Words from *vertere*

The word 'perversion' means wrong or bad use. It comes from the Latin *per* + *vertere* meaning 'to turn the wrong way'. 'The brutal perversion' of Stephen Wraysford's life in the extract from *Birdsong* suggests that the war is treating him like an animal (or brute) by turning his life away from what is normal. To 'pervert the course of justice' is to turn it away from what is fair and right. These days the words 'perversion', 'pervert' and 'perverted' are used most often of people whose sexual desires are turned away from what is considered normal.

Other words come from the Latin *vertere* with various prefixes. They include: 'invert', 'extrovert', 'advertise' and 'inversion'.

Exercise 9.8

Use the following words from *vertere* in sentences to make their meaning clear:

1 diversion

2 introvert

3 vertigo

4 subvert

5 transverse

6 versus

Words from *manus* and *opus*

Soldiers in training for the First World War often went on practice exercises called 'manoeuvres'. This is literally work done with the hands (from *manus* in Latin) but now meaning any job which is tricky and requiring special skill. 'Manipulate', 'manicure' and 'manufacture' all come from the same root. *Oeuvre* is the French word for 'work'. If we talk (in English) of the 'oeuvre' of a writer, musician, or artist, we mean everything he or she wrote, composed, made or painted – all that person's work. The Latin word for work is *opus*, and a writer's or composer's *magnum opus* is his or her 'great work'.

Exercise 9.9

Put these words into the spaces in the following sentences:

manipulative	operational	manoeuvring
manicurist	opus	manufacturing

1 British industry has moved away from _____ toward saleable services.

2 Because nail art is so fashionable my hairdresser now also works as a _____.

3 There were a lot of delays during the building but our school's new swimming pool is now _____.

4 _____ the car round the bend into our garage takes great skill and a lot of practice.

5 Each piece of music a composer publishes is given an _____ number to distinguish it from his or her other works.

6 If you try too hard to get other people to do what you want you will be accused of being _____.

Spelling revision

Make sure you can spell these words.

prophecy	memorial
condemnatory	charismatic
quarrelsome	horticulturalist
conservatories	technophobe
disappearance	guarantor

Revise the spellings and meanings of the words above.

Work with a partner. Take it in turns to call out the ten words above. Your partner should write down first the word correctly spelt and then its meaning. Score one mark for each spelling and one for each meaning so there is a total of 20 marks.

Make sure that you relearn carefully any that you get wrong.

Another ten words for revision are listed in Chapter 10.

Functions of language

Discursive language

In a discursive essay, it is important to write about the topic or issue in a measured and balanced way. This not a one-sided argument but a chance to explore a subject and weigh facts and arguments on both sides or from different perspectives.

The techniques of discursive writing reflect the fact that the views expressed need to be clearly reasoned and supported well by evidence so as to convince the reader of their validity. The techniques include:

- covering points for and against an issue or putting across two different points of view
- structuring these points either to cover all the 'for' points and then all the 'against' points or using each paragraph to address one pair of 'for and against' points
- using connective phrases at the start and within paragraphs to link ideas and show the direction the discussion is moving in
- using anecdote, facts or statistics to support each view expressed, e.g. 'able to raise an army of half a million men by the end of the year through volunteerism'
- formal language to give the views expressed authority, e.g. 'It is clear that...' or use of the passive, e.g. 'the war was precipitated by...'
- tentative language, to allow for other views to be considered, e.g. 'it seems as if', 'it could be said that'
- balancing language, which means alternative views may be put, e.g. 'Whilst some argue that ... others maintain...'.

The balance that is carried through a discursive essay usually continues right through to the conclusion, as the article by Stephen Badsey on pages 113–115 exemplifies.

Exercise 9.11

Write a discursive essay on this topic: 'War is always evil but sometimes necessary.' How far do you agree or disagree with this statement? Refer to and use the techniques of discursive writing introduced above and in Stephen Badsey's article on pages 113–115.

There are writing guidelines for this exercise in the answers. Look for the section at the end of the answers called 'Writing guidelines'.

Speaking and listening

1 Organise a class discussion about the rights and wrongs of war.

2 Prepare a presentation for a small group about what front-line life was like in 1916. Use the information presented in this chapter. You could also use books and the internet to supplement your knowledge and for sources of extra information.

3 Learn Wilfred Owen's poem by heart and perform it for the rest of the class.

4 Work in a group of three. Take the roles of Stephen Wraysford, Wilfred Owen and Professor Badsey. Discuss your experiences and/or express your thoughts about the 1914–1918 World War.

5 Read one of the books in the 'Extra reading' section of this chapter and tell the rest of the class about it.

Extra reading

All these books feature people living though wars in different countries at different times:

- *In the Morning* by Michael Cronin (2005)
- *Birdsong* by Sebastian Faulks (1993)
- *Charlotte Gray* by Sebastian Faulks (1998)
- *A Town like Alice* by Nevil Shute (1950)
- *Atonement* by Ian McEwan (2001)
- *War Horse* by Michael Morpurgo (1982)
- *Private Peaceful* by Michael Morpurgo (2003)
- *Sharpe's Eagle* by Bernard Cornwell (1981)
- *Gone with the Wind* by Margaret Mitchell (1936)*
- *Great Britain's Great War* by Jeremy Paxman (2014)
- *Testament of Youth* by Vera Brittain (1933)*
- *The First World War in 100 Objects* by Peter Doyle (2013)
- *The Ghost Road* by Pat Barker (1995)*

*Recommended for very keen readers and for those taking scholarship

Progress further

- Find out about the short life of Wilfred Owen. Read some more of his poems.

  Then listen to *War Requiem* by Benjamin Britten. It was written for the consecration of Coventry's new cathedral in 1962 because the old one had been bombed in the Second World War. Part of *War Requiem* comprises some of Wilfred Owen's poems set to music.

- Look at the website of the Commonwealth War Graves Commission (www.cwgc.org). If you have basic information about them, you can often trace relatives who fought or died in the 1914–1918 war.

- Research the history of the Royal British Legion. It raises money each autumn by selling poppies to help victims of war and their families. But there's more to it than that.

10 Marriage

Three sisters

Jane Austen sets the scene for her novel *Mansfield Park* by describing the marriages of three sisters.

About thirty years ago, Miss Maria Ward of Huntingdon, with only seven thousand pounds, had the good luck to captivate Sir Thomas Bertram, of Mansfield Park, in the county of Northampton, and to be raised to the rank of a baronet's lady, with all the comforts and consequences of an handsome house
5   and large income. All Huntingdon exclaimed on the greatness of the match, and her uncle, the lawyer, himself, allowed her to be at least three thousand pounds short of any equitable claim to it. She had two sisters to be benefited by her elevation; and such of their acquaintance as thought Miss Ward and Miss Frances quite as handsome as Miss Maria, did not scruple to predict their marrying with
10 almost equal advantage. But there are not so many men of large fortune in the world, as there are pretty women to deserve them. Miss Ward, at the end of half a dozen years, found herself obliged to be attached to the Rev. Mr Norris, a friend of her brother-in-law, with scarcely any private fortune, and Miss Frances fared yet worse. Miss Ward's match, indeed, when it came to the point, was not
15 contemptible, Sir Thomas being happily able to give his friend an income in the living of Mansfield, and Mr and Mrs Norris began their career of conjugal felicity with very little less than a thousand a year. But Miss Frances married, in the common phrase, to disoblige her family, and by fixing on a Lieutenant of Marines, without education, without fortune, or connections, did it very
20 thoroughly. She could hardly have made a more untoward choice. Sir Thomas Bertram had interest, which from principle as well as pride, from a general wish of doing right, and a desire of seeing all that were connected with him in situations of respectability, he would have been glad to exert for the advantage of Lady Bertram's sister; but her husband's profession was such as no interest
25 could reach; and before he had time to devise any other method of assisting them, an absolute breach between the sisters had taken place. It was the natural result of the conduct of each party, and such as a very imprudent marriage almost always produces. To save herself from useless remonstrance, Mrs Price never wrote to her family on the subject till actually married. Lady Bertram, who
30 was a woman of tranquil feelings, and a temper remarkably easy and indolent, would have contented herself with merely giving up her sister, and thinking no

more of the matter: but Mrs Norris had a spirit of activity, which could not be satisfied till she had written a long and angry letter to Fanny, to point out the folly of her conduct, and threaten her with all its possible consequences. Mrs
35 Price in her turn was injured and angry; and an answer which comprehended each sister in its bitterness, and bestowed such very disrespectful reflections upon the pride of Sir Thomas, as Mrs Norris could not possibly keep to herself, put an end to all intercourse between them for a considerable period.

From *Mansfield Park* by Jane Austen (1814)

Exercise 10.1

Read the extract from *Mansfield Park* and answer the following questions:

1 What were the maiden (unmarried) names of (a) Lady Bertram and (b) Mrs Price?

2 What did the youngest sister do which upset her family?

3. Explain in your own words the comment made about Maria by 'her uncle, the lawyer' (lines 6–7).

4 What do you learn about Mrs Norris's character from this passage?

5 What, in the context of this passage, is meant by (a) elevation (line 8), (b) scruple (line 9), (c) remonstrance (line 28) and (d) intercourse (line 34)?

6 This passage claims to be about the marriages of three couples. What is it actually about? Is there anything surprising which is not mentioned?

'Sonnet 116'

Let me not to the marriage of true minds
Admit impediments; love is not love
Which alters when it alteration finds,
Or bends with the remover to remove.
5 O no, it is an ever fixèd mark
That looks on tempests and is never shaken;
It is the star to every wand'ring bark,
Whose worth's unknown, although his height be taken.
Love's not Time's fool, though rosy lips and cheeks
10 Within his bending sickle's compass come;
Love alters not with his brief hours and weeks,
But bears it out even to the edge of doom.
If this be error and upon me proved,
I never writ, nor no man ever loved.

William Shakespeare (1609)

Exercise 10.2

1 What does Shakespeare mean by (a) 'love is not love / Which alters' (lines 2–3) and (b) 'Love's not Time's fool' (line 9)?

2 How many mentions are there of love and loving in this sonnet? What do you deduce from this?

3 What is the sonnet's main message? Support your answer with quotations from the poem.

4 How effective do you find the final rhyming couplet and what do you think it means?

5 Shakespeare personifies Love in this sonnet. What does he tell us about the figure of Love?

Why an arranged marriage 'is more likely to develop into lasting love'

They are seen by many as business deals that have little to do with love.

But arranged marriages are far more likely to lead to lasting affection than marriages of passion, experts claim.

5 According to research, those in arranged marriages – or who have had their partner chosen for them by a parent or matchmaker – tend to feel more in love as time grows, whereas those in regular marriages feel less in love over time.

And within ten years, the connection felt by those in arranged marriages is said to be around twice as strong.

10 Relationship experts claim this is because arranged matches are carefully considered, with thought going into whether potential partners' families, interests and life goals are compatible.

This means they are more likely to commit for life – and to stick together through rocky patches.

Those who marry for love, on the other hand, tend to be blinded by passion and 15 so overlook these crucial details.

When the going gets tough, they are more likely to view the situation simply as a natural end to their romantic dream – a way of fate telling them something is wrong with the relationship.

With soaring divorce rates and record numbers of single-parent households 20 in the West, researchers suggest it is time to rethink the Western approach to love. Harvard academic Dr Robert Epstein has studied the subject of arranged marriages for eight years, looking at the approaches taken in cultural groups including Indian, Pakistani and Orthodox Jewish.

25 He has interviewed more than 100 couples in arranged marriages to assess their strength of feeling and studied his findings against more than 30 years of research into love in Western and arranged marriages.

His work suggests that feelings of love in love matches begin to fade by as much as half in 18 months, whereas the love in the arranged marriages tends to grow gradually, surpassing the love in the unarranged marriages at about the
30 five-year mark.

Ten years on, the affection felt by those in arranged marriages is typically twice as strong.

Dr Epstein believes this is because Westerners leave their love lives to chance, or fate, often confusing love with lust, whereas those in other cultures look for
35 more than just passion.

He said: 'The idea is we must not leave our love lives to chance. We plan our education, our careers and our finances but we're still uncomfortable with the idea that we should plan our love lives. I do not advocate arranged marriages but I think a lot can be learnt from them.

40 'In arranged marriages, thought goes into the matching. In the West, physical attraction is important. But people must be able to distinguish lust from love. Strong physical attraction is very dangerous, it can be blinding.

'In the West marriages are easy to get out of. But in arranged marriages, the commitment is very strong. They get married knowing they won't leave, so when
45 times are harder – if they face injury or trauma – they don't run away. It brings them closer.'

Francine Kaye, relationship expert and author of *The Divorce Doctor*, added: 'There is an awful lot to be said for arranged marriages. They are determined to make it work.

50 'I have seen in arranged marriages in the Orthodox Jewish community that the parents very carefully look at compatibility – it is not left to chance. They do their homework on their characteristics, their values, morals and life goals.

'It should be pointed out that arranged marriages work because culturally marriage is seen differently. We have a very romantic view of marriage. Theirs is
55 more pragmatic.

'There is a downside to arranged marriages though – no matter how pragmatic you are in choosing a partner, there always
60 needs to be chemistry.'

From an article written by Paul Bentley and published in the *Daily Mail* (2011)

Exercise 10.3

1 (a) Where does Dr Epstein work?

  (b) Who wrote *The Divorce Doctor*?

2 Which communities favour arranged marriage?

3 What research has Dr Epstein conducted?

4 Why does Dr Epstein think arranged marriages are stronger than conventional ones? Use quotations from the article to support your answer.

5 Summarise Francine Kaye's views about arranged marriage.

6 How strong do you think this is as a piece of journalism? Is there anything else the journalist could usefully have included?

Writing practice Exercise 10.4

1 Write a story called 'Marriage of True Minds'.

2 Write a sonnet about an emotion using Shakespeare's 'Sonnet 116' as a model. Try to use the same rhythm and rhyme scheme.

3 Write your views about arranged marriages for a magazine article.

4 Describe a wedding that you have attended.

5 Imagine you are Mrs Frances Price. Using the information you are given in the passage from *Mansfield Park* on pages 123–124 – and adding to it in any way you wish – write to your sister Mrs Norris telling her about your life and what you think of her views.

6 Write on the subject of marriage in any way you wish.

7 Imagine that you are an older person who is married. What advice would you give to someone who is thinking of marrying their partner? Remember to include personal experience to reinforce your arguments.

> There are writing guidelines for task 3 (writing an argument) in the answers. Look for the section at the end of the answers called 'Writing guidelines'.

Did you know?

These facts relate to the writers or topics featured in this chapter:

- 'Sonnet 116' is one of the 154 which Shakespeare wrote and which were published as a book-length sequence in his lifetime – unlike the plays which were not published until after his death.

- Jane Austen, who lived in Hampshire for most of her life, was buried in Winchester Cathedral in 1817.

- Fewer British people now choose to marry than at any time for hundreds of years.

- Arranged marriage, which requires the consent of the couple concerned, is completely different from 'forced marriage' in which couples are given no choice.

Exercise 10.5

Research and note three separate facts to add to the list above. They should relate to marriage or to the writers and other topics touched on in this chapter. You should be able to summarise each of your facts in a single sentence.

◯ Grammar and punctuation

Pluperfect tense and past participles

Past participles (see Chapter 9) are used with two forms of the past tense.

They are used with the perfect tense. For example: 'I **have** noticed'; 'they **have** eaten dinner'. The auxiliary verb is in the present tense.

The further past, or pluperfect tense, uses the past tense of the auxiliary verb and pushes the action back one stage further in time. For example: 'We **had** finished'; 'you **had** left'. The implication of this is usually that the pluperfect action happened before something else in the sentence.

For example:

> She **had** rung her mother **before** she left home. (The whole sentence is in the past tense, but she rang before she left and the tenses make that clear.)

> I started the car **after I had** checked that there was petrol in it. (It is all in the past tense but one action takes place before the other, although in this case they are expressed in a different order.)

The past tenses of the verb 'to have' are often contracted with their pronoun subjects giving 'we'd', 'I'd', 'they'd', 'you'd' and so on.

Exercise 10.6

Use the pluperfect and other forms of the past tense to complete these sentences. Underline each use of the pluperfect tense.

1 Once Vicky _____ she _____.

2 Ben _____ but he _____.

3 After we _____ we _____.

4 Before you _____ we _____.

5 I _____ before I _____.

6 My grandparents _____ they _____.

Revision

Below are the remaining points about good English written for journalists by a newspaper editor. The first ten are in Chapter 9.

11 Contractions aren't necessary and shouldn't be used.
12 Don't use no double negatives.
13 Eschew ampersands & abbrevs.
14 Eliminate commas, that are, not necessary.
15 Never use a big word when a diminutive one would suffice.
16 Kill all exclamation marks!!!
17 Use words correctly, irregardless of how others use them.
18 Use the apostrophe in it's proper place and omit it when its not needed.
19 Puns are for children not groan readers.
20 Proofread carefully to see if you any words out.

Exercise 10.7

Take the above sentences one by one and explain the points that the editor is making.

◯ Spelling and vocabulary

Words from *coniungere*

The 'career of conjugal felicity' mentioned by Jane Austen for Mr and Mrs Norris means 'happy married life'. She deliberately used slightly pompous vocabulary here because it's the sort of thing Mrs Norris herself would have said. And, since it was a practical marriage of convenience – because of the money rather than one based on love – it probably wouldn't have been particularly 'felicitous'. Jane Austen, as so often, is being ironic.

'Conjugal' means 'joined with'. It comes from the Latin word *coniungere* (to unite). 'Conjunction' and 'conjugate' come from the same root. When two stars or planets move to a position which from Earth looks as if they are touching (as in an eclipse) they are said to be 'in conjunction'. We also get words such as 'junction', 'joint' and 'disjointed' from *iungere*.

Coniumgere is spelled with an 'i' because Latin does not use the letter 'j'.

Exercise 10.8

How many different meanings can you think of for the word 'joint'? List them. Then use a dictionary to help you think of more.

■ A solar eclipse occurs when the moon passes between the Earth and the Sun

Exercise 10.9

For a bit of spelling and vocabulary fun, see how many words you can make from the letters of DISJOINTED. Each of your words must:

● contain an 'e'

● have four letters or more

● not need a capital letter.

Stationery and stationary

Most couples getting married want wedding 'stationery' which means paper goods and must not be confused with 'stationary' which means standing still. There are two ways of remembering the difference:

● Stationery contains an 'e' for envelope.
● Stationary comes, like the words status and statue, from *stare* ('to stand') in Latin and the root is an 'a'.

Exercise 10.10

Words which sound the same but which have different meanings or spellings are called homophones.

Find, or work out, ways of remembering the difference in spelling and meaning between these five easily confused pairs of homophones. Make a note of the meaning of each.

1 compliment   complement

2 councillor   counsellor

3 elusive   illusive

4 gorilla   guerilla

5 alter   altar

More spelling revision

Exercise 10.11

Work on these ten words with a partner until you both know all the meanings and spellings.

monologue	openness
pseudonym	mnemonic
pneumonia	quarrelsome
bewildered	embarrass
rheumatism	clamorous

◯ Functions of language

Language for newspaper reporting

Modern newspapers include many different sorts of articles, but news stories – factual accounts of things that have happened – are still their central purpose. Paul Bentley has the job of reporting to readers of the *Daily Mail* that research has been conducted into arranged marriage, and how well it works, by an American academic.

When informing readers, journalists writing news reports are traditionally expected to answer the questions Who? What? Where? and When? at the beginning of their pieces. That is why a typical news story opening might be:

> The Queen distributed silver Maundy coins to 85 men and 85 women – signifying her current age – at a service in Westminster Abbey yesterday.

Who?   The Queen

What? She gave Maundy money to 85 men and 85 women.

Where? In Westminster Abbey

When? Yesterday

When a journalist attempts to explain a story in further detail, they will deal with the questions How? and Why?

> The 85 men and 85 women are retired pensioners who have been invited in recognition of their community service, and will receive purses in a tradition that dates back hundreds of years.

How?   Pensioners are invited to receive the coins.

Why?   The ceremony continues a long-standing national tradition.

Most journalists work to a code of practice – a set of agreed rules – which says that they must not confuse news with opinion. That is why news stories are usually on pages clearly headed 'News'. Other pages, on which journalists analyse the news and state their views, have headings such as 'Comment', 'Views' or 'Analysis'.

Paul Bentley:

- uses a headline which summarises what the article is about
- summarises the article in the first three short paragraphs; you could stop reading after paragraph three but you would not have fully understood his message
- keeps his paragraphs short – often just one sentence
- summarises what Epstein says
- uses direct quotes from both Epstein and Kaye.

Exercise 10.12

Write a short news article (up to 300 words) for a broadsheet newspaper about anything you wish. Be as direct as you can. Summarise the news first. Use the rest of it to give more detail. Use some of the techniques demonstrated by Paul Bentley.

◯ Speaking and listening

1 If you have people in your class from different cultures, organise a session in which you tell each other about wedding customs in your families.
2 Discuss marriage in a small group. What do you think is the best age to get married and why?
3 Discuss your views about arranged and forced marriage. Make sure you are completely sure about the difference between them.
4 Work with a partner. Rehearse a shared reading and perform it to the rest of the class.
5 Invite into school a speaker from Relate, a charity which works with couples whose relationships are in difficulties. Question the speaker about Relate's work.

> There are writing guidelines for this exercise in the answers. Look for the section at the end of the answers called 'Writing guidelines'.

6 Interview a married couple who have been together for a very long time (grandparents perhaps?) about how things have changed since they were first married. You might also quiz them about what makes a long and happy marriage.

Extra reading

These books all have marriage and ideas about it at their centre:

- *My Dad Is Ten Years Old* by Mark O'Sullivan (2011)
- *Love, Aubrey* by Suzanne LaFleur (2009)
- *Tamar* by Mal Peet (2005)
- *The Photograph* by Penelope Lively (2003)
- *Second Honeymoon* by Joanna Trollope (2006)
- *Good Wives? Mary, Fanny, Jennie and Me 1845–2001* by Margaret Forster (2001)
- *Small Island* by Andrea Levy (2004)
- *Marie and Pierre Curie* by John E Senior (1998)
- *The Way We Live Now* by Anthony Trollope (1875)*
- *Vanity Fair* by William Makepeace Thackeray (1848)*
- *Mansfield Park* by Jane Austen (1814)*
- *Love in a Headscarf* by Shelina Zahra Janmohamed (2009)
- *(Un)arranged marriage* by Bali Rai (2001)

* Recommended for very keen readers and for those taking scholarship

- When a couple have been married for 25 years they can celebrate their silver wedding anniversary. The 50th wedding anniversary is called a golden wedding. Find out what the 15th, 20th, 30th, 35th, 40th and 60th wedding anniversaries are called. Why were there more golden wedding anniversary parties than usual in 1995?

- Both partners in the following marriages were famous, either because they worked together or because they each achieved something separately: Leonard and Virginia Woolf; Sidney and Beatrice Webb; Pierre and Marie Curie. Find out what they did. Can you add some living couples in which both partners are achievers?

- The traditional ending for a story is a wedding and a happy life 'for ever after'. Think of *Snow White*, *Cinderella*, *Jane Eyre*, *Pride and Prejudice* and many others. How realistic do you think this is? Think about, and discuss, whether a wedding is an end or a beginning.

- Anton Chekhov wrote a play called *Three Sisters*. How many stories, plays, etc., can you find, or think of, which, like *Mansfield Park*, feature a trio of female siblings?

- Read and discuss the following leader column, 'Date expectations', published in *The Times* on 5 January 2006. Who was/is Cupid, Lady Bracknell and Thomas, Annie and Clarabel? How far are the 'rules' of good journalism, set out earlier in this chapter and the last, applied?

Date expectations

The humble mouse has replaced Cupid's quiver. Last year, more than 3.5 million single Britons used an online dating service to find romance. Instead of directing inquiries on comparative pulchritude to the mirror on the wall, 65 per cent of all those in search of a compatible mate turn now to the screen on the desk.

5   The internet's reputation as a panderer needs some burnishing. To most people, chat rooms mean chat-up rooms. But some of today's internet chaperones are as strict at protecting the reputation of their matchmaking and the virtue of their charges – mostly female – as any Victorian matron. They begin with a catechism as searching as any of Lady Bracknell's inquiries:
10   likes, dislikes, values, beliefs, favourite films and horrible habits. No chatting is allowed unless the protocol is observed, the psychometric profile completed and often the fee – real, not virtual, cash – paid up-front. Then, with suitable caveats, the lonely questor on love's tortuous path may be vouchsafed a personalised selection of three tantalising e-mail addresses.
15   Pictures come later, though lookist sites – beautifulpeople.com or gorgeousnetwork.com – will post your portrait only if found attractive by a panting team of superficial selectors.

An online search has huge advantages. It is quick. It is open at any time in any
place (even, surreptitiously, from the office). It carries none of the hangdog
20   associations of the mournful dating agency or the drink-sodden sleaziness
of the bar. And it can refine the field as narrowly as you wish: gardeners,
Catholics, redheads, Chelsea fans or even steam enthusiasts. Thomas, meet
Annie or Clarabel.

From an article published in *The Times* (2006)

The tools of poetry

Poets use tools to create poems in the same way that a wood carver uses a chisel to shape a carving or a chef uses a whisk to beat egg white. For the poet the raw material is words and the tools are the devices he or she uses to shape the words. And just like any other sort of device, every item in the poet's tool kit has a name. Some of these have been mentioned in this book and/or in *English for Common Entrance One*. They are referred to in the related answer books too.

You need to know the names of the tools and what exactly they do in order to be able to write about poetry accurately and well. So here, in summary, is a list of the main ones with examples taken from the poems used in this book.

Alliteration – the repetition of the same letter or sound, usually at the beginning of neighbouring words. You can also use the adjective **alliterative**:

   ...downward smoke, the slender stream

   (From 'The Lotos-Eaters' by Alfred Lord Tennyson: see pages 71–72)

Assonance – the repetition of the same vowel sound (not necessarily spelt the same way) in neighbouring words. You can also use the adjective **assonant:**

   Plump unpecked cherries

and the repeated:

   Come buy, come buy

   (From 'Goblin Market' by Christina Rossetti: see page 19)

Caesura – a break in a line of poetry. This was usual in Latin poetry and still exists in some English poetry. It is usually marked with two vertical lines when analysing poetry.

   Admit impediments; || love is not love

   Which alters || when it alteration finds,

   (From 'Sonnet 116' by William Shakespeare: see page 124)

Consonance – words close together that use the same consonants (the vowels may differ).

Alone and palely loitering

(From 'La Belle Dame Sans Merci' by John Keats: see pages 5–6)

Enjambement – the continuation of meaning from one line of poetry into the next so that the sentence (as it were) does not end at the end of the line:

Then all smiles stopped together. There she stands

As if alive...

(From 'My Last Duchess' by Robert Browning: see pages 43–44)

Metaphor – the comparison of one thing with another by pretending that the thing described really is what it is being compared to. Like personification or a simile (see below) a metaphor is a form of image. The adjective **metaphorical** and the adverb **metaphorically** are useful too. Metaphors are not *literally* true. The man in the example below is not actually dying in water. He has been gassed:

I saw him drowning

(From 'Dulce et Decorum est' by Wilfred Owen: see pages 112–113)

Onomatopoeia – the use of words to imitate sounds. A single word, like 'sneeze', can be onomatopoeic, but poets also often put words together **onomatopoeically**. In the example below the repeated hissing or sibilant (see 'Sibilance' below) and 'z' sounds suggest the sound of the insects.

hushed with buzzing night-flies

(From *Henry IV Part 2* by William Shakespeare: see page 98)

Personification – the giving of human qualities and abilities to non-humans. Poets often personify things as a way of describing them. It creates an image or picture in the reader's mind:

The winds were lovesick with them

(From *Antony and Cleopatra* by William Shakespeare: see pages 55–56)

Sibilance – the repetition of hissing 's' sounds (not necessarily spelt the same way), including 'sh', within neighbouring words. You can also use the adjective **sibilant**:

a seep silent all summer

(From 'November' by Ted Hughes: see pages 29–30)

Simile – a comparison of one thing with another which makes it clear that it is a comparison by using the words 'like' or 'as'. It is yet another sort of image.

> sodden as the bed of an ancient lake

> ...

> Like hammered lead

(Both from 'November' by Ted Hughes: see pages 29–30)

Many of these devices are used over and over again in the poems we study in this book. To make sure that you have understood – and to 'fix' your learning – go back and look for examples of each device in each poem.

But remember that the important thing – once you've identified the device – is to work out what it's there for, why the poet used it and what it adds to the poem ... and that's the real joy of poetry!

Index